When Children Think

WHEN CHILDREN THINK

THINK

Using Journals
to Encourage Creative Thinking

by

GABRIEL H. L. JACOBS

TEACHERS COLLEGE PRESS
Teachers College, Columbia University

Manufactured in the United States of America

To Binnie

Contents

Foreword

This book is a description of some techniques for developing children's creative thinking which I have worked out as a teacher at W. T. Page Elementary School in Montgomery County, Maryland. Most of these methods are based on the journals of new ideas that the children in my classes have kept.

For the last nineteen years, as a student, a teacher, and a principal, I have worried about how to teach children to think. We have reached a time when the mere knowledge of facts is no longer sufficient for holding many jobs. It is much more important to be able to use information in a productive and creative way — and this involves thinking.

I have always felt inadequate in the face of all the articles, speeches, and other injunctions saying that children should be taught how to think. I had had doubts about my own ability as a teacher, feeling my intellectual equipment might be deficient, that there might be a great deal of information about how the mind works that I did not know about, and that I might need more teaching experience to divine the secrets involved.

The answer to how to teach thinking seems to be immensely complex and simple at the same time. We really do not know how, although there are some indications. The indications we have would point to having to define thinking as the opposite of recalling information already stored in the brain. Obviously both are mental processes but they have different values in different contexts. Here, some definitions are in order. My own definition would combine the following: problem solving, artistic creation, writing skills that convey a true feeling of authenticity to the reader, and newness for the person doing the thinking. This quality of newness does not preclude making use of information and ideas previously acquired. This is not a complete definition but there is little literature in the field that helps. Most of the studies in the field of creativity have to restrict the definition so that measurements can be made. One definition by E. Paul Torrance which I found particularly useful was: "the process of sensing gaps or disturbing missing elements; forming ideas or hypotheses concerning them; testing these hypotheses and communicating the results, possibly modifying and retesting the hypotheses."* Josephine Arasteh† in her review of the literature on creativity has considered imagination synonymous with creativity. That sits well with me. Imagination, originality, fantasy, curiosity, uniqueness, and divergent thinking, are among some of the terms used to describe creativity. It is not the purpose of this book to review the literature, but from my study of it, it appears we have a long way to go to find out more about creative thinking.

If we knew exactly how to develop creative thinking, could we agree on exactly what results we wanted to produce? If we knew how, would we not be doing it already? To state the obvious, the human mind is a highly complex organism and the problem is not simple.

In the course of my education (and I mean education in the broadest sense of the word — formal and informal), I have come to value the use of the mind as the most important of man's activities. It bothered me that I was so inadequate at training the mind. My view of my role as a teacher was that I was being paid to do exactly that, although the taxpayers might have been convinced that my only job was to teach subject matter. (The narrowness of that view of the teacher's role does not seem as prevalent today as it has been.)

With the idea of teaching thinking on my mind for many years, I developed a number of techniques aimed at developing children's thinking. All of them had very restricted application, but at least I was doing something. The problem still preyed. Then about four years ago a number of things I had been thinking, reading, and talking about began to jell into the idea of having the students keep journals of their new ideas. It was nebulous at first, and when I tried it on the first class, what happened in the first few months was not what I had in mind at all. It took some development on my part before my children hit pay dirt. My children were very patient with me while I grew and learned. Their patience in the early days was particularly remarkable because I was asking them to do something that they could not visualize. Of course the fact that I couldn't visualize it either did not help. I was asking them to do a certain kind of job which neither they nor I knew much about.

It is hard to pinpoint exactly where one's ideas come from. Joe Howard's becoming my principal was probably the immediate stimulus to trying out journals of new ideas. Working with Joe, I got to feel that my limitations as a teacher

*E. Paul Torrance, *Guiding Creative Talent* (Englewood Cliffs, New Jersey: Prentice-Hall, Inc., 1962), p. 16. Reprinted by permission.

†Josephine Arasteh, "Creativity and Related Processes in the Young Child: A Review of the Literature" (Bethesda, Maryland: Child Research Branch, National Institute of Mental Health, [n.d.]), p. 3.

were my own rather than those imposed externally. It was a humbling experience. I loaned Joe my copy of *How Children Fail* by John Holt and his reaction to it, as well as his reaction to some of my more irregular classroom procedures, convinced me that in his school there was an atmosphere where one could experiment. My readings of Holt, A. S. Neill, and psychonanalytic literature, and the atmosphere of real concern with experimentation in education at my alma mater, Goddard College, were probably some of the major contributing factors to developing the journal of new ideas. There were also my own observations about how I developed new ideas and my many discussions and arguments with my very aware and brilliant wife, Binnie.

The book that follows is made up of many quotations from children's journals of new ideas. I have used the quotations not only to illustrate the techniques I have described, but for their own very interesting qualities, and to show the kind of thinking children in the nine to twelve year old range can produce. Rather than try to fit the children to the book, I have tried to fit the book to the children. Their writing has given direction to much of what I have written. I have been learning from them and there is no reason why the book shouldn't reflect this.

Most of the children's ideas are not new to mankind but they are still exciting to read. They have verve and a quality that conveys the fun of thinking and it is for this reason that the last chapter is composed mostly of journal entries that I wanted to share with you. I hope that you get the same intense pleasure from reading them that I do.

The kids have found and corrected most of their mistakes and there was very little need for me to do much with their entries. I have made some corrections, although in many cases I have left their mistakes in because they add to the flavor of their work.

The children whose entries are in this book ranged in age from 9 to 12 years old, and were in the fifth and sixth grades. Their backgrounds vary from very poor to upper middle class. Page is an integrated school whose black children also range from very poor to upper middle class. Some of our children, who are foster children from very difficult family situations, have come through with top notch thinking.

Of the twenty-six children in my class last year, twenty-two have entries in this book. No effort was made to get a broad representation. All of them produced a quality of entry equal to those included. Lois Weinstein's class had thirty-five children and fourteen are represented. Bert Lloyd's class had twenty-six, twelve of whom are represented. There are entries from other classes as well, but the greater proportion of entries from my class stems from my being more familiar with their work.

Since completing this manuscript a little over a year ago, I spent four weeks this past summer as a demonstration teacher at Montgomery County's Language Arts Workshop teaching a heterogenous group of 9-12 year olds. My approach was somewhat more relaxed during the summer than with a regular class. The total number of entries specified for this group for the whole session was eighteen. Twenty-two of the twenty-seven children produced eight or more entries of excellent calibre during the four weeks. The remaining five produced several entries of a good calibre. Of the twenty-seven children only two are represented (their entries were particularly illustrative of certain points) as I had already completed the manuscript when I taught at the Workshop.

I have changed the names of the child authors so as not to embarrass them. No two authors have been given the same name. Dates of writing have been put in. All of this was to enable the reader to use these internal clues to satisfy his curiosity and trace the development of a child's work.

Seven of the children's entries appeared in my article entitled "When Fifth- and Sixth-Graders Think" in the October, 1968 issue of *Childhood Education.*

There comes a time when one has to thank the people who have assisted in the preparation of a book. My first thanks must go to the children who have kept journals of new ideas. They have been patient and extremely helpful in copying over many of their journal entries for my use. Lil Carleton, Ken Egloff, Bert Lloyd, Sandy Sher, and Lois Weinstein are some of the teachers I am indebted to for their comments and suggestions, and for making available to me their children's journals. I particularly want to thank Bert and Sandy for giving me repeated opportunities to test out my new ideas about journals, and hear theirs. I am also indebted to them for taking the trouble to write up their thoughts and experiences with journals so that I could include them.

My thanks must also go to Alan Dodd, who, when I was first working with journals, suggested the possibility of writing a book about them.

My wife, Binnie, has read and reread this manuscript an infinite number of times and has come up with a number of invaluable suggestions. Where the book falls down it is because I was too pigheaded to listen to her.

I

A Journal of New Ideas

A journal of new ideas was to be kept by each child in several classes at Page School. On the first day of school, I told the children that thinking and using the mind were the most important things we could do. I said that all of us have new ideas, exciting things happening to us, and things we get curious about each day. These were the things to describe in the journals.

Each child was to write up his new ideas in his journal five days a week. He could write about any subject, and choose any five days of each week. The form of the entries could vary. An entry could be a description of a new idea, a question followed by the reasons for asking it, an explanation of why the child was curious or enthusiastic about something, a question that excited him with his guess at an answer, any combination of the above, or even a form not mentioned. It could also include diagrams. Each day's entry was to be about something new to the child and was to be complete.

I asked the children to come up with new ideas and share them with us that first day. They heard me read exciting journal entries that had been written by my students the year before. I made a spectacle of myself in my enthusiasm for new ideas. They got the message.

The kids were being asked to think creatively on a daily basis. They were not being asked to do problem solving in the narrow sense of using the problem solving and symbolic logic techniques. The important thing that I was trying to get the children to do was to think creatively in all areas of their lives. Certainly some of the journal entries below reflect a broad range of thought.

Conrad: Fall
    We were talking about the entries and I looked up and saw that the wind changes in direction. I think that the Earth rotates and causes wind like when you're riding in a car with the windows down it causes wind.

But how does it change in direction? I don't think the Earth rotates straight. I think it rotates in a wobbly form. I also think that is what causes changes in direction.

Susan: March 16

A design is really something! I mean people always say, "I only like realistic paintings." But if you go up in an airplane you can look down and see many beautiful things but they will look fake and small. So it just goes to show that a painting can be beautiful without being realistic!

February 17

Sometimes when I go down in the lunch line I see people every day but some I have an extra large feeling to say hi to them. There is a boy I don't know his name but he seems to give me the feeling he's pushing me to say a word or two with him. This situation would normally happen with your opposite sex. But I don't understand what is going on when this happens.

Bonnie: June 4

The way companies exaggerate their products is sickening. I'm watching T.V. and this ad comes on about Sunshine Rinso. It (supposedly) brightens clothes so bright you have to wear sunglasses. The next thing you know a poor woman goes out to buy some of the product and she can't tell any difference in the brightness of her wash!

The companies are always saying 30% more or 15% less. But what does a housewife want to know about percentages? All she wants is a better toothpaste, detergent or something that will do the job better and when she hears the commercialist saying 50% more she's expecting a very big difference. What does she find out? The only difference she can see is that her wash is a little bit whiter. One tiny speck.

Why don't they just say it straight out so the buyer knows what he's getting.

Boy! What a world!

Charles: March 14

Last night when I went out I noticed a car under a street light.

I noticed something you usually don't see.

The steel of the car had a circling pattern like this:

This really made me wonder.

Then I went into the store. There I looked at some heavy machinery like power saws, drill press, and other things.

The steel on these also had a circling pattern.

This really made me wonder.

Could it be that because the steel is ground smooth, that the steel gets a circling pattern?

Maybe the circling pattern in the steel just comes naturally and when it is ground and polished it shows up more.

Certainly there are some questionable assumptions in these entries. There is also some very good questioning.

My purpose in having children keep journals of new ideas was not to have them summarize and parrot things they had learned. It was to have the children become conscious of what a new idea is, learn how to develop an idea (think it through more and observe more if necessary) and write it up in a coherent way. Since many parents judge the quality of children's achievement by the quantity of their output, the journals also served the useful function of showing them that their offspring were doing real work by having daily writing and composition practice.

To produce this kind of very exciting thinking the kids and I had to have conditions that would not inhibit creative thinking. We had to have the support of the school administration, which might be faced with parents complaining because their children put down something inaccurate in the journals. Joe Howard, principal of Page School, was willing to cope with such problems, and was enthusiastic about the experiment. As far as I know, there were no parent complaints.

The first year when my kids started journals they were describing events of the day rather than new ideas. Until the children and I understood more clearly what new ideas were and how they could describe them there was a time of floundering. After the children were writing very exciting entries Joe Howard and I had an interesting discussion. He told me that when they first started and were writing about events, he couldn't understand why I was so enthusiastic about their journals. Had he said so at the time I might well have dropped journals then. Trust and faith are essential to this kind of creative thinking. The teacher has to feel his principal trusts him and the children have to feel that their teacher is trustworthy so that their minds can range free and they can write about the things that are important to them. The entries below show this very pointedly. The first entry by Bonnie was at the beginning of the year:

Bonnie: September 14
On my ring finger the skin is white where my ring usually is. There is a red lump with black instead of light hair. Why is this? The reason it might be white is the sun can't bleach it. The red bump is probably an insect bite. You may think this is a stupid thing to write about but it interests me very much.

Had I agreed with her then she might never have come up with an entry of this quality:

Bonnie: April 25
People are making things easier to do. One example is that I.Q. tests would need alot of people to check answers but to make the work easier they have developed checking computers.
I say (using the example above) when you think you may be making things easier you are actually making it harder. The reason I have behind me is that to make the checking easier you have to develop a certain type of sophisticated computer and then be able to run it.
I bet alot of people disagree with my idea and now that I think of it I'm beginning to wonder about the idea myself.

The following two entries also reflect a great deal of trust by the child. Both are written by children from another class whose teacher, Bert Lloyd, is using the journals of new ideas.

Gladys: December 2
Last week I took a visit to my old neighborhood to visit my girlfriend. As the car drove into Pine Hills (that's my old neighborhood) I felt like I wasn't wanted. Just like you feel when you were playing with someone you get mad at them, then you saw them, but you wanted to say to them, "I'm sorry, can I play with you?" But right before you say that, that's how I feel. I don't know why but I just feel that way. Is it just your mind? Or I haven't been there in such a long time.
Do you know Mr. Lloyd? Have you experienced that feeling when you were young? Or even now as a man. Is it your feelings inside of you?
I think these kinds of experiences occur most on grown-ups. Not in a way that I experienced but maybe in an experience to do with relatives or deep true friends and especially a man's wife.

Ilse: April 19
When I was a little girl I would say a lot of lies and my mother would believe me. Now I hardly ever say lies but my mother says that I should stop saying lies because I lie more than I ever did before. I wonder why people always think the opposite of what it really is.

At the age of eleven would you have been willing to say or write those things for a teacher or adult to read? When children are free to say this kind of thing they are also free to do some very sophisticated thinking and learning in all areas.

It seems to me that getting kids to produce results like these certainly contributes to the development of their creative thinking abilities — not that we know much about creative thinking. What we do know seems best expressed in the negative: creative thinking does not usually occur on demand or after a five-minute exercise in logical thinking. Considering a problem and trying to restrict your thought to that specific problem may inhibit creative thinking. Creative thinking may occur at seemingly unlikely times and long after we have been mulling over the problem.

Ilse: June 10
Why is it that when you try to think of something you can't think and when you are relaxing your mind is racing? I've thought of this as a journal entry but I've never found the right words for it. Really, I wasn't relaxing when I thought of this. (But anyhow)

What seems obvious to an adult may represent real creative thinking on a child's part. Creative thinking cannot be narrowly restricted to arbitrary limitations which teachers frequently set. If the child attempts to stay within narrow bounds, whether set by himself or by the teacher, creativity will be stifled. In many areas of academic work we are not looking for creativity, but in the journals we are. This means that the child is likely to come up with some ideas that may be distasteful to the teacher. Some entries might seem disrespectful of adults or of their pet notions.

Our knowledge of the world around us is still very limited. When a child makes a discovery it may seem elementary to us. We should see that the importance of a new idea is relative. What is important when he makes a discovery is that the child is continuing the process of profound thinking. A child's ideas may be simultaneously naive and sophisticated, and his discovery of something new to him is as important in enlarging his world as our advances in science are to us.

Donald: October 26
Why is the earth's core hotter than the rest of it? I should think it would be colder from no sun. But maybe like the sun our planet has hot burning gases. This would explain volcanoes. Hey, if this is true we can't or better not put any A bombs down too deep or we'll blow up.

Craig: May 23
My sis said that when you go to sleep your eyes go up in your head. I know this is true but if they go up in your head how can an M.D. see your eyes to say they go up in your head?

Scott: December 19
If something contracts when it gets cold if you got something cold enough would it keep on contracting until there wasn't any space left between its atoms?

Grace: October 25
Today I was wondering why countries who need money do not just print some more. What I am trying to get at is when a nation owes another country money and does not have it, it orders the men who work the printing machine. Why don't they do that? Wouldn't it solve some financial difficulties? Of course, only a high person could give this order, but still, why wouldn't it work? I think it could solve a lot of difficulties.

Margaret: December 21
They are having a holiday truce in Viet Nam. What I can't understand is if they can have a truce now, why wouldn't they stop the war all together?

Stephen: December 14
My father took his truck to the mechanic early this morning to be fixed. He was told by the man that he would have it fixed the same day. The truck was waiting to be fixed all day, but the man never tried to fix it.
Why do children get punished when they tell a lie but big people lie all the time?

II

Thinking about Physical Phenomena

Physical phenomena hold a compelling interest for children, and are a recurring theme for them to write and wonder about. Many of the children write only about physical phenomena and many who write about other things keep coming back to physical phenomena. The sophistication of their thinking frequently astounds me. For instance, I am very much of a space buff and every space shot that is televised becomes our subject matter for that time. Charles's entry below on the automatic sequencer for firing rockets shows great depth of thought about the problems of firing a rocket:

Charles: September 14
    Today I wondered about the two second launch window. Mr. Jacobs told us that everything happened so fast that they had to program the procedures on tape but how could they program it that fast on tape?
    Maybe they do it as fast as they can and then double or triple the speed at the launch.

The following entry by Ernest also reflects profound thinking even though the assumption he based his entry on is erroneous:

Ernest: May 2
    Mr. Jacobs today read a whole lot of journal entries. One said that they didn't understand the difference between magnetic north and regular north. Well this doesn't pertain to that, but in a way it does. I was thinking about some of Mr. Jacobs' maps of Long Island Sound. There, they said that the difference between magnetic north and regular north was 6½°. Well, on some of the topographic maps that I have, of the area down here, they say that the difference between magnetic north, and regular north is still 6½°. Objection is, we're about 200 miles further south than Long Island Sound. Wouldn't this mean a smaller difference than up in Long Island Sound?

I think this entry is wrong. On one of Mr. Jacobs' topographic maps it has a total difference 13°. I'm totally wrong. Please ignore all of this. No comments from the peanut gallery please.

I praised him highly for his reasoning.

Genuine praise and respect for a child's thinking is an absolutely necessary part of the classroom atmosphere if results like these are to be achieved. The children have to feel that it is all right to make a mistake and still have their ideas recognized as excellent thinking.

The body of man's knowledge not only increases but it also changes. We used to think of our accomplishments in science as representing a solid body of knowledge. These days it is not unusual to find that what we thought of as a solid fact is no longer considered to be one. I am very reluctant to point out to a child that he is wrong because I may well be wrong. On the other hand by agreeing with a child I may reinforce his error. By telling him that he is right or wrong I am closing out his further learning and exploring. Bonnie's entry is a good description of this:

Bonnie: December 4
I think and I realize that great thinkers and scientists were helpful to mankind even if they had ideas that were later proven false. This is shown in one like this. Aristotle didn't believe the atom or atoms idea. But, he got men to thinking of his idea and thinking of more plausible ideas. Thus, discovering the atom and advancing in science. This is only one example. Mankind might be nothing if it didn't have these people.

Once a child has thought and written about something he is more aware of it and does more observing and thinking about it.

Cheryl: March 10
Today when I went to the Wax Museum I noticed a wax hand holding a dollar bill. On a sign it said that each person could take one. Of course none would want to miss an opportunity like this.
I tried to take the dollar in the wax hand except I couldn't and none else could. It was so real that you couldn't take the dollar. It was sticking out of the wax hand just like you or I were holding a dollar bill but was only an optical illusion.
This is just like people in the desert imagining an oasis. You can imagine how happy they are when they see water until they walk up closer and find out it is an optical illusion.

March 28
In one of my previous journal entries I had written about an optical illusion and how it happens. Just today I was riding in our car in the front seat. As we were driving along the highway the car seemed to be on two lanes of the highway. It was very strange to me. I told my mother about what I saw and she said that the angle I was looking at our lane from is what made me see it this way.

Now since this happened I am beginning to understand what an optical illusion is. It is something you concentrate on and imagine that the thing is really there. It is also the way you are looking at something for instance, the story I just mentioned. These are all things that are part of an optical illusion.

Frequently children change their minds and in later entries correct what *I* *thought* were wrong conclusions. This happens even though I have never said I thought they were wrong. The following two entries by Yolanda are excellent illustrations of this and of her increased sensitivity to a question thought of previously.

Yolanda: April 28
. . . But I am wondering what insects really live for. They have such a short and boring life and they really don't accomplish anything except laying eggs that will hatch into insects that will have boring lives. People and some animals at least live a longer life and have something to do in their life.

May 24
Today I was thinking about something I wrote in one of my Mar-Lu-Ridge* entries. I said that insects have nothing to live for and are just useless. But without hardly thinking I realized that insects are the food for birds, frogs, toads, and other small animals. Bees make honey. And bees also help pollinate flowers. When they are trying to get nectar for a flower they brush pollen off of the anthers onto the stigma. Each piece of pollen grows a tube down to where the seeds are. It pierces it and that is like fertilizing it.

Ernest wrote this entry when he was in my class:

Ernest: May 5
. . . I was, after a while, thinking about the insect study. Mr. Wood said that insects cannot think, but all of what they do is burnt out in nerve patterns. Well, sometimes when a human is sick, they have spasms, or convulsions. During this period they act like insects and this instinct makes them react in certain ways to certain things. I believe that this instinct is like a fire engine. When a person is unconscious, this acts as a defense. In a sense, humans have nerve patterns burnt out all over them, but can only use them in an emergency when it has no other ability.

*Mar-Lu-Ridge in the Catoctin Mountains is a Lutheran camp that the Montgomery County Public School System rents for the purpose of outdoor education. Sixth graders are taken there to spend a week in residence studying those things which can be best studied out of doors. Insects, ecology, forestry, animal communities, history using unwritten sources, and map and compass work are among the subjects studied. Little emphasis is placed on camping skills, but living together in this context provides many social benefits. (See also p. 44)

He came back to visit me the following year and he handed me this entry which he had just written:

Ernest: January 10
The most interesting new idea I have had this year is a combination of several facts, including:

Source
Mrs.
Crawford

A. You shiver in the cold.
B. You have involuntary muscles in your brain.
C. When you move, you oxidize.
D. When you oxidize, you release heat.
E. You have a "thermostat" in your brain.

The idea goes as follows: One morning I was out in the extreme cold. I had not dressed warmly, and I was not moving, so I was shivering. I knew that when you move you have to oxidize food, and that releases heat, so I thought that shivering might be involuntary action, caused by a drop in temperature in your body. This then forces you to shiver, and to shiver you must oxidize energy, releasing heat, which will slowly warm you up . . . .

Ernest is the kind of child who is going to do this kind of thinking whether or not a vehicle such as a journal is provided for him. However, it may be that having a journal as a thinking vehicle and having organized this kind of thinking for a year, he will be an even abler thinker. I hope it is giving a start to others who will keep on doing this kind of work. Unfortunately, too much of our approach to learning is still taken up with the learning of a body of knowledge rather than with using the mind to *use* knowledge. As our information retrieval systems get more sophisticated, as they show every sign of doing, learning specific bodies of knowledge is not going to be as important as being able to put knowledge to use.

Much of the children's excellent thinking has already been done by man, but this should not detract from the impressiveness of their thoughts. In some cases the ideas may be totally new. In the following entry Tim has invented something which may have been invented already. I don't know. It may be new to mankind:

Tim: February 28
Today I asked Mr. Jacobs about geographic north and magnetic north. He said that there was one more north pole but he couldn't remember its name. I think that a two pronged needle could point to both simultaneously but it would have to be adjusted constantly as you travel.

The entry below by Douglas is not new to mankind but reflects very searching thought on his part:

Douglas: May 13
   Today my father told me that you can't get tetanus germs in you unless
you have an unopened cut. The tetanus germ can't live with oxygen or air.
   This could mean that there are other types of life on other planets such
as the tetanus germ and maybe even developed bigger.

Sometimes the children's observations of physical phenomena take an unintentionally humorous path as in Ceceile's entry:

Ceceile: December 20
   Why do women switch when they walk? Everyday I see Miss Sher
walking down the halls and she always switch(es) when she walks.
   Every skinny woman switches when they walk. I wonder why?

My first reaction to this was that she meant *swish* and not *switch*, but after
rereading it, thinking about it, and watching Miss Sher more closely when she
walked down the hall, I am sure she meant switch. The children in struggling for
new ideas manage to come up with very vivid imagery.
   As you can see from many of the journal entries quoted so far, the children
do not restrict themselves to school subjects. The two entries that follow are
from ardent baseball players who have described some things in the area of
science using baseball as their starting point.

Charles: May 25
   Today I had a hard time catching fly balls at baseball practice.
   The trouble was that I couldn't judge how far away or how high they
were.
   If I remember right, there was a clear sky today with no clouds.
   I think this may have been a factor in my misjudging those flyballs.
   I think this because – well just look up at the sky on a clear day and
try to judge distances.
   It's pretty hard isn't it?
   Now if you hit a baseball up into a clear blue sky and try to judge it,
you've got problems.

Bernard: June 1
   Last year when I was playing baseball I hit a home run. I didn't try to
in the way of killing the ball. Then I tried killing the ball and I struck out.
I wonder why? I thought that when you try killing the ball you take your
eyes off the ball and get nowhere. But when you don't try killing the ball
and follow it all the way in you can get a hit.

The entry below raises a deep philosophical question about some of our
formal disciplines and is probably a good example of using specific knowledge
for deeper thinking.

Craig: April 24
   One day I was thinking about science and social studies. This is what I
was thinking about. Social studies was in the middle of (during the ice age)

time and science was in the beginning of man. I wondered where science began and where social studies started. I think science began with when the earth started. I think social studies began when man was fully developed.

And what was the middle of this called?

What do you think?

Here is a series of entries which I feel show excellent thinking.

Douglas: February 16

Today I didn't learn anything. But I did remember something that I had learned on another occasion. This was when I went to a movie one night. I noticed that when the scenes or colors changed from place to place so did the beam of light. There were bright beams which were probably the bright colors, and there was also almost no beam at all but yet there was still a beam. The beams didn't have any color to them except for bright light and darker light.

Louise: April 26

. . . I am not sure what the difference is between magnetic north and true north. We also used our maps, and found that some of the things on the map were incorrect. You'd have to make a map every single minute if you wanted to be correct . . . .

Yolanda: April 18

Today we went to a planetarium. I have been to planetariums so many times that I really didn't get any new ideas. But I was watching the machinery (or equipment) and I saw that the planets and stars were put onto the ceiling with light. (like a flashlight) At least it looked like that's how it was done. The part I can't figure out is why the light would not spread out like a flashlight. But maybe a flashlight is made to spread out light and the equipment in a planetarium is specially made not to somehow.

Martha: February 24

Today I learned that you don't need a magnifying glass to see how different each flake of snow is. While I was outside I stuck my glove out and picked up a few snow flakes. I saw that if they don't land close together you can see the different patterns very clearly of each snow flake.

Gwen: April 12

Today I wondered why it is that when you are watching television you are tired, so you go to bed, but when you go to bed why aren't you tired? I thought this was because of the light on the television. When you left it you weren't seeing the light.

Alan: October 19

I was riding home from Hebrew School. It was pouring buckets of rain. I heard over the radio the humidity was sixty-nine. I wonder how it can rain when the humidity isn't one hundred.

Keith: April 14

Why is it when you are in the bathtub you have rings around you, but when you look under you you don't have any rings? Why does this happen? I think the rings are under you at first and then the water floats the rings to the side and then it makes rings.

Craig, in some of his entries which you have already read, has tried to put his finger on some things that are very difficult to get hold of. I am not sure I understand this one but it seems to me there is something here that is an important part of a child's developing ideas about himself and the world around him:

Craig: May 11
    I was thinking about time. I thought that a pencil was time. I say this because a pencil is made of wood and wood comes from trees and trees

were a part of time. And if you drew a picture like this   time is

still going into this around and around. Time, I think, is no way to tell when something happens, it is a way to think that time is, something is happen(s)ing.

I could not make a few corrections needed on that entry because I was not sure I understood his meaning. However, he is reaching out strongly. Many of the children get involved in trying to understand what time is.

Susan: January 26
    It seems like the older you get the faster time goes. When I was a real little girl about 4 or 5 I used to dig in the dirt sunup to sundown. The days were so long and playful having fun all the time.
    Nowadays I am eleven almost twelve and the days are so short and you work every second. The statement the older you get the faster time goes is so true. I just hope that when I get as old as my parents, time won't go even faster than now. Because "It is already too fast!"

III

Children's Thoughts about Interpersonal Relationships and Themselves

For this is the journey that men make: to find themselves. If they fail in this, it doesn't matter much what else they find. Money, position, fame, many loves, revenge are all of little consequence, and when the tickets are collected at the end of the ride they are tossed into the bin marked FAILURE.

But if a man happens to find himself — if he knows what he can be depended upon to do, the limits of his courage, the positions from which he will no longer retreat, . . . the secret reservoirs of his determination, the extent of his dedication, the depth of his feeling for beauty, his honest and unpostured goals — then he has found a mansion which he can inhabit with dignity all the days of his life.

James A. Michener, *The Fires of Spring**

Depth of thought, perceptivity, and brilliance are not restricted to thinking about physical phenomena and school subjects. Inevitably, much of the kids' thinking is about themselves, their relationships with others, and man's relationship to man. It is part of finding themselves.

The entry that follows puts into words something we are all familiar with.

Bonnie: May 21

I've been observing, and the thing I've been observing is that people try very hard to make certain specific impressions on one (or more) certain specific people.

It's really funny because a person may make one kind of impression on one person and then make a completely different kind of impression on someone else.

One thing that shows this is the following: alot of the time when my younger sister has a friend over I act like a big shot. I would think this is because I want other kids to think I'm tough (translation: great). On the other hand I find that whenever one of my big brother's friends comes over I act such that a person would think I'm really nice. Another reason I think someone (I) would act like that is that I'm a girl and he's a boy so I would naturally act nice.

Another example is the following: a friend of mine who is usually acting big came over to my house because she was going somewhere with us. I was playing catch with my older brother and when she came I introduced them. She was as sweet as an angel. That probably happened because of the same reason I behaved the way I did when my older brother's friend was here.

My guess is that a person knows they should make a certain impression on certain people.

Maybe they have some type of instinct or intuition that says, "Hey! be a big shot to this person" or "Be sweet as an angel."

Many of the children, particularly the girls, are worried about becoming teenagers.

Bonnie: January 1
The thought of growing up has me scared for some reason that seems hard to explain. The reason I have is that I'm scared to go through the different stages of every person's life. The stage I'm mostly afraid of is being a teenager. I've seen alot of teenagers and some of them think they're the best brains. They act like they know everything. They seem to be so ignorant and stuff like that. The thing that has me really scared is that I would become one and when I think about it, it gets me all upset.

There is a great deal of puzzlement about what boys and girls find attractive about the opposite sex.

Craig: March 20
I know women put makeup on to look good. But I think this is wrong because if a man is on a date and looks at this girl and says, "What a pretty girl," when they get married the man looks at her without any makeup and almost dies. So I think this is wrong. The only trouble is that women don't understand this.

Susan has combined her worries about growing up and what the boy and girl relationships are about:

Susan: October 7
Sometimes when my sister comes home from a party and even other girls, they'll sit and cry their eyes out for a boy. How come the girl has to cry her eyes out and the boy just sits and relaxes around? Maybe it's that the boy is worrying while he's sitting down. But honestly I don't know the real boys' side but anyways I don't care. Besides it isn't my problem yet.

Later in the year she was still very concerned with the problem and wrote many more entries on the subject:

Susan: January 31
I asked my sister what she talked to her girlfriends about. She said,
"Naturally *BOYS* stupid." Well that's finished. Then I asked this other boy
named C. B. what he talked to his friends about. He said, "What else
GIRLS is the only thing to talk about." I will tell you what both sexes talk
about as soon as they know and I find out.

                                                         February 2
You must think I am a nut always talking on this subject but anyways
I'll go on.
I have found a new system how you know when you like a boy alot. I
will use different names than the incident.
Example:
You could say oh I like Ted a whole lot. So the next day you see Ted
and if your stomach does not fall you know you don't like him. Then if
you see Steve and your stomach does fall you know then you like him. So
if you walk past a boy or a girl and your stomach does fall you know then
that, that's the one.

Ceceile seems to be simultaneously naive and sophisticated in her approach to
the subject. In any case she has described some of the more usual boy and girl
situations with a great deal of accuracy:

Ceceile: April 27
Today I wondered why boys "eye" girls when they see them in bathing
suits. The boys wear them so can't they "eye" each other instead of girls.
They act as if they have never seen a girl's shape. On me, they always
"eye" me out no matter what I wear!

                                                          April 28
Today I wondered why girls get all the attention when they walk or
look really good. There's a boy on my block named Lester who looks at
me all the time no matter what I wear.
He moved but every evening he comes back to our neighborhood just to
see me. I wonder why. Does he want to "eye" me more?

                                                           May 4
Today when I went over to my grandmother's house, my two cousins
were playing a band. All of a sudden these two girls kept trying to get their
attention. They did it again and they did. They kept on talking out loud
by calling their names but when they called their names they kept walking.
I wonder why.

                                                          May 31
Today I wondered why boys get so excited when they're around a girl.
Last night at the ice-cream truck Ralph, Lester, and a couple other boys
were outside with my sister and my friends. (I was too.) Then the boys
started to get excited with us girls and it really was a jam. What makes us
so important and special to them?

                                                          June 7
Today when I broke up with Lester it seems to me I still liked him.
Then a week later, he started to hate me. I wonder why.

Not too long ago I broke with Fred Rowley and now he hates me and just can't stand me. I wonder what makes boys do this. What do you think?

June 12

Today Sheila told me that she likes this boy named John in the fourth grade. Then she told everyone to ask this boy did he like her and he said, "No!" It can really make a girl feel terrible when a boy doesn't like them but if a girl doesn't like them they will make them like them. I wonder why. It doesn't feel terrible to a boy but it can make a girl feel bad.

Since our children go to junior high schools in the seventh grade, these speculations about boy-girl relationships are inevitable.

Ceceile is also experimenting with finding out who she is. She is working out a new role as a girl and what is most amazing to me is that she has described it so well and allowed me to read it.

Here is a problem that is more and more common in our mobile society. Betsy gives her entry a twist at the end that really drives it home:

Betsy: September 7

I never knew how hard it is to leave your friends until I had to do it. All of a sudden I'm in a new house, a new neighborhood, and everything changes, different friends, different teachers, and a different school. It feels terrible.

I've walked to and from school with my girlfriend for six years. I've played with her an awful lot, and miss her. Every year at Rose Valley Elementary new people came into our school, but I didn't know what they had been through except for now. I hope I like it here.

In the following entry, Cheryl has managed to verbalize something that very few of us, adults or children, are able to put a finger on as well as she does:

Cheryl: April 4

When my brother and I fight my father and mother get angry at us. They just don't understand that it is part of a game. The object of the game is to get the other person real mad and get them to chase after you. Sometimes you might not get to a room fast enough so you tell the person you are sorry, but you are really not. The reason you go to the room is to stop the person from hitting you. In a way it is not a game, but a teasing session. All these things that I mentioned at the top are the way you play the game, but parents don't feel that way. They feel it is a time for crying since they also feel that you will get hurt. I wonder why parents feel this way. I guess it is because their hair is turning gray and they feel like an outsider with this younger generation. Of course this might not be true with your parents, but it is with mine.

Certainly anyone who has had brothers or sisters or has more than one child knows exactly what Cheryl is talking about.

Teasing is a concern of many of the children as is seen in another entry on the subject.

Sandra: March 4
   Today I got mad at my girlfriend because she pushed me down in the mud. She acted as if nothing had happened. Then when she saw I was mad at her, she came over and started laughing at me. I didn't want to talk to her. What I don't get is if people want to still be friends why do they do all these mean things to you? I'm going to find the answer too.

Of course the children speculate about their relationships with their parents. The entry below is somewhat unusual, but speculating about parents is not.

Ceceile: May 8
   Today when my mother and I were fussing, I got real smart with her by saying, "Don't worry about it," and she hit me! Then I hit her back and she said, "Don't you hit me girl!" and then she hit me back. I wonder why? She hits me but she doesn't want us to hit her back. We have feelings too.

Betsy is also touching on several things that involve her own search for who she is:

Betsy: October 17
   I think there should be a lady president because who says men are smarter than women? Maybe there are some men smarter but they're also women smarter than men. I think that if there were two that I liked the best that were a woman and a man I think that I would pick the woman because then I could get a *little* idea what it would be like. You need more than one women president though, to find out really what it would be like you need around three. All three would be different so you will get three different ideas. The same goes for a man president. You need more than one man president, but at least three, to judge men presidents. I don't know who is running for president but I hope someone who is smart, sensible, and brave wins it.

Notice how carefully she has thought this out. Her comment about needing three women presidents "to find out really what it would be like" is a very mature one.

Karl has made a comment that unfortunately even those of us who know better don't fully respect:

Karl: June
   At the end of school kids are always happy or sad about report cards.
   Well, when I was in the car with my mother and I was not happy about my report card, but still I thought about it and I think other people think that it is everything, but it is only school not your personality.

The following entry is without benefit of much punctuation, grammar, or correct spelling, but as you can see from her writing, this child does some excellent thinking. If one were to insist that in every entry her spelling and grammar be perfect I doubt that she would be learning to do this calibre of thinking on paper. Knowing her, I don't think she would write much at all if she were faced with the constant discouragement of having to correct every other word.

Connie: June 17
    When your parent talk about your childish behave you get mad sometimes as sound as you turn around one of your parent is doing someting childish like when you are playing with paper and the teacher tell you stop then the teacher will call you up to his desk and he will be playing with paper. Why do the teacher do things like that.
    My guess is that the teacher wants to act big and they like to play with paper. He or she would get in trouble because they were playing with paper. Mr. Jacobs told me not to play with something and he turn around and was play with it.

Connie has something there. In fact, the reasons she gives as motivation for her teacher may not be so far off. One has to be prepared for journal entries that strike quite close to home if one has provided an atmosphere of real freedom for the kids.
    Another aspect of finding yourself is detailed in this entry of Frank's:

Frank: December
    Over the Christmas holiday I was wondering what it would be like, if my father had not married my mother. I will give you my version of the story. I can imagine it would be dull. You can imagine what it would be like being a nothing. You could not do anything. You wouldn't be you. You would be out of this world. I could not stand it.

Charles has provided us with a typical situation in life:

Charles: February 6
    Last night when I was taking a shower my brother came in and asked me if he should do one thing or another.
    This puzzled me. What he asked me is not important. It's why he asked me.
    I wonder why little kids want people to make up their decisions and as they grow older they want people to leave them alone.
    If I knew this, I would be a great psychiatrist!

In the following entry, Betsy evokes a very vivid picture of what happens to her when she reads:

Betsy: September 12
    When you read a book you try to think of pictures in your mind, like if a book says Jack and Bill were in the woods, you think of woods, with Jack and Bill in it. Someone might have their grandma's woods, and some-

one else might have the woods in back of the school (in mind). When I read Hardy Boy books I think of them in my Grandma's woods. Then all of a sudden there's a picture of the opinion of the illustrator. Her thoughts are completely different from mine. In every book there is a picture, maybe not on paper but in your mind.

Betsy's entry above not only explores another facet of herself but it also explores how the mind works.

IV

How Do I Think?

In this chapter many children are quoted on the subject of how they think thinking works. Because they have been expected to produce five journal entries a week, with a new idea in each, they naturally become concerned about finding ideas. These ten to twelve year olds have fascinating theories on how they get ideas and how they think. They do not have the long experience of experiencing that we do. As a result, their noting of thinking sensations is sharper than ours and it may be well for us to take some hints from them about how the mind works.

One of the first things the children seem to notice is how their ideas come. The most common theme is that new ideas come when they are relaxing. Many children mentioned that the bathtub and bed are the places where they get new ideas. Many mention that when they are trying hard, they do not get ideas, but when they relax, they do.

Theresa: January 10
Today I was wondering how people get new ideas. When I get my ideas I relax and they just pop into my head and then I write them down. Other people get their ideas different ways but I don't see how they just pop into my head. I also wonder why and how one minute you have an idea and the next minute you forget it.

Gwen: March 1
Sometimes when I try to think of a journal entry I think and think but I can't think of anything, but when I relax, watch television or something I get a journal idea. Maybe this is because I am just thinking I've got to get a journal idea, I've got to get a journal idea, and I'm not really trying to think of a journal.

Sandra: March 6
This morning I woke up around 2:00 A.M. and all of a sudden I started

23

getting all these ideas for my journal. When I woke up again this morning I couldn't remember the ideas. Why do you always think of entries at funny times? I can't even remember whether the entry I'm writing now is one of the ideas. That's how funny it is.

Bernard: June 6
    Today when I wanted to play but I couldn't go out until I had written a journal. I started thinking with nothing on my mind but play so nothing came to my mind. Then I realized I was getting nowhere. I gave up. I sat down and stopped thinking. I started thinking but not real hard. I got an idea.

These children all seem to be talking about ideas popping into their heads when they are relaxing. In the following entry, Gwen has come up with a different thought about how ideas come:

Gwen: April 20
    Today I wondered how book writers can think of such good things to print in their books.
    If they get an idea how can they remember it?
    I thought maybe they would write their ideas down and if they forgot something, they would wait until they thought of something else.

Cheryl has come up with her own explanation for these strange happenings:

Cheryl: January 12
    When I was getting ready to go to sleep I made sure I was all ready for school the next day. It seemed that everything was in order. When I got in bed I began to think what I needed. I remembered then I needed comics, a magazine, and a book. I began to wonder why I thought of this now instead of before. I also thought of a journal entry in bed, but couldn't think of one when I needed one.
    These things are very strange to me. The only answer I could think of is because your mind must be concentrating so hard it makes you forget to do things like these until you're in bed relaxed. Relaxing and not being so nervous must be the main reasons why you can and can't do a better job.

Another area there is a lot of speculation about is how the mind works. Yolanda, for instance, is curious about how the brain stores information:

Yolanda: April 5
    I didn't get any new ideas today but I was wondering about some things. One question I asked myself was how a clump of . . . (your brain) can think and store information? I think that it has something to do with brain waves and cells. But what I really was wondering about is "how?" I don't think anyone knows.

Then Sandra comes up with other approaches to the subject:

September 21

Today I was wondering. Why do people wonder? My guess is that somebody isn't sure about something and keeps on thinking about it. They can't do much about it just sitting there. Some people think funny things. Sometimes I wonder what Mr. Jacobs is thinking. Sometimes he looks like he's ready to do something to you, and he comes out with the happiest things. I love to wonder about big things.

Sandra: September 29

What really is a mind? I know its something that controls the body, but how does it know just what to do at a certain time?

Why did God make minds different? Why aren't they all alike? A mind to me, is one of the hardest things to understand in life.

Keith's analogy may well be closer to the truth than we know:

Keith: March 1

What makes you think? How do you think? Does your brain help you think? I think when you were born you had a sort of vacuum cleaner but it picked up words. And that is how you think.

Because there has been emphasis on thinking and new ideas, some of the children begin speculating about kinds of thinking. They wonder about the difference between what they have been doing all along and the thinking they are expected to do for their journals.

My guess is that the single most difficult thing for children to learn to do when keeping journals of new ideas is to identify a new idea. Once they can overcome this hurdle and begin to see and feel what a new idea is, they acquire the habit of recognizing this kind of thinking. This is the breakthrough that takes a while for many children. Many different approaches need to be tried to have the child come to see what a new idea is. When a child says he cannot think of new ideas, I say to him, "Describe why something is exciting to you," or "What are you most curious about?" or "Describe why you like to do some particular thing more than anything else." Sometimes this works. Once the child has tried a couple of things along these lines, he is often caught up in the spirit of new ideas on his own. He stops following my suggestions and begins to come up with ideas by himself. Sometimes this does not work, and additional personal conferences, demonstrating exciting entries on the overhead projector or reading them aloud, conferring with another child, or reading his friends' entries may help him get the feeling. It can be quite discouraging until he does, but it is well worth the effort.

Often the children are quite surprised to find that many of their new ideas are just ordinary thinking which they have carried a little further. It is really a process of becoming conscious of what they are thinking about and deciding what they want to think through further and describe.

They are also puzzled by the charge to them to think. When they reflect about this some of them come to the conclusion that what they do all the time is thinking.

Charles: December 20

Today when it was snowing, just before we left school Mr. Jacobs said that we didn't have to write any entries over the Christmas holidays, but we still had to think to get some entries.

I think all the time. At least I think I do.

But when I write Journals I think it's a different kind of thinking that I use because if I could write using my normal thinking all the books I could buy wouldn't hold one year's entries.

Geraldine: December

I have often wondered about thinking. What I wonder is, can you ever have a completely blank mind? (Apart from hypnotism and sleep) I really don't have a clue what the answer is, because I don't think there has been a time when my mind was completely blank but I'm not the only person in the world.

Betsy: September 9

You couldn't be able to stop thinking no matter what. You can say OK, I'm not going to think. You would only be thinking not to think. Every second of your life you're always thinking.

Bernard: November 23

Today as I was writing my journal I wondered why Mr. Jacobs makes us write journals?

He told me and the class that it would help us think faster.

But why does he want us to think when we all already know how to think?

In connection with how we think some children become concerned about forgetting.

Gwen: January 3

Today I wondered what makes a person forget things. When I learn something in school, I usually don't forget it, but when I do something or something happens to me I forget. I thought this was from my not having as much experience when I do something in my subjects. In my subjects I study about it several times. I don't study about something that happens to me or I do. I may do the same things several times and forget them, but not very often.

Kenneth: October 12

Last year I was at math and the teacher asked a question that was new to me. I started trying to answer him. I wonder why every time someone asks a question you don't know the answer to them but when you are doing something else the answer comes to you.

Theresa: April 24
    Today I was wondering why when you're talking about something that
you know about and somebody asks a question you can't say the answer
fast enough. This just happened to me last night. My father was talking
about the sun, the moon, and the days of the year. My brother and I were
listening and my father asked us a question. I knew the answer but it
seemed that it was on the tip of my tongue but I couldn't say it. I don't
understand why this happened. I think it might be that you know what
the answer is in your mind but you're so busy thinking of the answer (in
your mind) and trying to babble it that you can't say it.

Two boys have written some very sensitive entries on a subject that makes a
writer's job tough.

Craig: March 3
    I have been wanting to write this entry for a long time because I
thought that you would not like it. Well here it is:
    That you could really not express things in words. Because if you wrote
a sentence, somehow there is a feeling in it. Because one day as I was
trying to write a sentence with a feeling in it and I could not.
    How do you write a feeling?

Craig seems to contradict himself in the entry above but he has managed to
get a tenuous hold on something that is very important. Glenn writes on the
same subject but with a different approach:

Glenn: May 11
    Can you write a feeling? I say that you can't because some things are so
beautiful and ugly you don't have words for them. If I had a girlfriend and
I had a feeling towards her it would be hard to write her. You wouldn't
know what to say.

As you might expect, children are interested in dreams and déjà vu.

Susan:
    Sometimes things happen to me and they will repeat again. This
happens real often to me. I'll see something and it will repeat. It's a real
funny feeling! I'm going to take a real wild guess at what happens. You
may dream about it or think about it or it could happen. But I'm going to
contradict myself it couldn't necessarily have happened because I never
knew Ellen before and things like that have happened with her in the
pictures.

Theresa: January 6
    Today I was wondering why sometimes when you do something you
feel as if you've done that thing before but you're not really sure. Take for
instance a dream I had last night. When I woke up I thought I had that
dream before but I was not really sure. I don't understand this at all.

                                                                            April 6
    Today I was wondering why sometimes when you get real excited you

feel as if you were in a dream. This happens to me a lot and when it does I wonder whether I'm in a dream or not, but it seems that when I get yelled at or something I know I'm not in a dream but I wish I were. Why?

Another topic of interest to children is man's intelligence in the past. They even talk about the tool being the developer of intelligence rather than man developing intelligence to make the tool.

Glenn: April 14
    In my study of Greece I found out that men started a way of thinking. I wonder how can these men be so smart when we think they are dumb? Men these days, would be dumb if they didn't have the tools we have today. So that shows people that man needs the tools he has today or bye-bye.

Bonnie: February 8
    A question I shall bring up was brought up before in a discussion and it is, "Were the cavemen more *intelligent* than we of today?"
    I'm not saying that caveman was but there is a very good possibility he might have been. I've heard that since 1940 our knowledge has doubled but I wonder if that is as much as cavemen did. That is, from the caveman time to the Stone Age time caveman may have progressed that much.
    The reason I think this is so is because by the time the Stone Age came man had developed a great deal. He had (I think) metal tools, crops, crude clothing, an organized built home made of straw, etc. He also began to use his brain logically in capturing animals, in building, and in plowing fields. One of their greatest achievements was developing communication between themselves.
    I wonder if we could do these things if we were in his position. The things above may seem primitive, but without them developed we would have a tough time, because it seems most of the things we do and know are based on these things.

These ideas are new to the children, not necessarily to mankind. Children need to get in the practice of getting new ideas in order to come up with things that are new to mankind. Of course, when doing our everyday work most of us aren't expected to come up with ideas that are new to mankind but we are expected to come up with new ideas for accomplishing our work. If the children do not shatter the world with revolutionary concepts at least they will have practice in what will become an increasingly important part of the work of the world. Charles's entry touches on this nicely:

Charles: September 20
    Today I had a new idea. Just because someone has a new idea [before] it doesn't mean it isn't new to me.

After all, how many of us come up with something totally new? Frequently, don't we pull little bits and pieces of information and ideas from various places (most of them from sources we do not remember), put them together, distill them, and come up with something new and useful?

There comes a time for many of the kids when they become very excited about getting new ideas, and some have communicated their thrill in their entries. The next entry gives this feeling.

Gwen: September 23
Today while I was thinking of a new Journal entry I started to write something about the sky. Then I thought the stars are millions of miles away. What's behind these stars? I asked my father about this and he said it was God's kingdom. Again I thought the sky never ends. I was confused but all I know is if I keep thinking like I am now I'll never finish.

The following series of entries by Bonnie reflects her enthusiasm for thinking and shows how her thinking developed during the course of a year. Bonnie is a child very much concerned with the importance of intellectual matters who thoroughly enjoys playing with ideas. (For those who might get the wrong idea she will be ruthless in taking advantage of you if you play basketball against her.) It is interesting to see her reactions to having to come up with ideas. She is one of the few children who has written entries about the joys and sorrows of journal-keeping, although many have described them to me. Bonnie is one of those children who developed a system of hoarding ideas until she needed one for an entry.

Bonnie: October 19
Why is it that the ideas I think of usually come in spurts? It always seems that at one time I'm full of ideas then suddenly I can't think of anything. I suppose that either my mind needs to rest every now and then or that it doesn't discover or find different things to ponder about all the time but finds them in bunches.

December 19
I have been getting stuck for new ideas lately and it's a queer thing because I can usually think them up just like that. I think a reason might be that I can't think of new ideas because my mind isn't relaxed. I need a relaxed uncluttered mind to think freely and well so I can come up with good ideas and that's exactly what I don't have.

December 22
Sometimes I wish Mr. Jacobs wouldn't have us write new ideas because when I think of something and it keeps happening I really want to know why. One thing is the irritation I get on my ring finger when I wear my ring. It always happens. When I wear my ring I get the irritation, then if I misplace my ring the irritation disappears. Later when I find my ring and wear it again the irritation comes back. This happens so much it almost drives me batty! On the other hand I like to write ideas because it gets me thinking and I come up with what I think are good ideas. You know, I never realized how one could do thinking like that until this year.

December 30

All of the Christmas vacation I've been racking my brains for new ideas and nothing shows. I wrote before (I think I wrote before) about how I could think new ideas up the best when I'm relaxed, but now I'm beginning to doubt this idea since I haven't been able to think of any ideas. I've had a lot of time, but I may not have been relaxed. Come to think of it, it may just be that because every time I try to think of one I get a funny feeling in the back top part of my head. It gets so frustrating, it's terrible and it drives me batty!! (Help!!!!) The mind is the greatest masterpiece of the universe (in fact, of everything) and I wish I might be able to take a trip through it and study every bit of it. Like my being made small enough to go in a submarine that could travel through the mind, just like some movie. The mind is so great, a mystical thing that . . . oh, gee whiz I can't seem to express myself it's so wonderful but someday I hope to find out something about it. It's such a wonderful, mysterious, thing that it itself seems to be questioning about itself. It has to be because that's what controls me. It's such a wonderful, mystical thing it is utterly confusing and that's the way I find myself now. Help, help, help, help . . . !!!

(I must apologize if you find this entry confusing because I was quite excited and I may have expressed myself poorly, I'm very sorry.)

January 19

One thing that really has me awed is the effect this writing of new ideas has on me. You never really seem to be able to realize that you could do this type of thinking. These ideas seem to give me a bit of pleasure or more so it seems to relax your mind. . . . I never thought I could do such thinking until this year and I think if I stopped writing down my new ideas I would stop thinking them up.

January 27

Recently I've been wondering what it's like in your brain when you have a dry spell in terms of thinking of entries. If there seems to be a pressure on your mind it could be very exhausted and a bit careless. It might not be exhausted at first (when it just ran out of ideas) but after your brain has been searching hard for an idea it becomes exhausted when it can't find an idea it gives up, then suddenly an idea pops up and the dry spell is over. Or it might just be that your mind needs a rest and when you try and force it to think it seems to fight back.

March 12

You may find I have not written my fourth journal for the week of March 6th (this entry being the third for that week). It may be I haven't written this entry because I find myself bored. It may sound silly to you that I might be bored but before you think about it I want to say I'm not sure in what *way* I find myself bored. I think I don't want or don't feel like writing journals because I'm bored with the writing. I think I don't like to write journals because writing entry after entry makes me tired and I just get sick of writing. Mind you, I didn't say sick of thinking ideas up but of writing them down. Mr. Jacobs has said that writing an entry can take only 5 minutes to write and isn't really hard to do. My problem is that when I write I need time to choose words to express my ideas and feelings. This is sometimes hard to do correctly and the reader may misinterpret. Also when I develop an idea I like to explore every crack and corner that I can or in other words I like to really get involved in an idea and be able to find a lot of different ideas about it in my mind. This way I can write an entry which I enjoy doing and that excites me. I also hope that the reader can get involved himself. This may or may not answer the question I brought up about not writing entries because I feel I may have gotten off the subject. As to wandering off the subject I think it is because I have gotten so involved in this entry that I just about don't know what I'm writing. Many times I have talked about being really involved and really being excited by an entry and thought you might like to know this is one of those entries. I would also like to mention that at the beginning of the entry I found myself tired and I wanted to drop writing journals because of how I disliked the writing. But now a completely new feeling has come over me. Maybe it is because I have gotten a load off my shoulders. The load won't be off completely until I find out what Mr. Jacobs or more so the reader thinks of this entry. I'd like to say that this may be the end of a very drearysome dry spell because I find I don't think I'll mind writing entries. Now I think a journal of new ideas is a helpful pal because my journal has taken a big load off my shoulders by my being able to write this entry and express my feelings. I almost think a journal is human.

May 16

The day when we were having our journal discussion (with Miss Sher's class) Mr. Jacobs asked the question, "What is the difference between normal thinking and journal thinking?"

I think that journal thinking is just normal thinking extended off to more extremes.

When I say extremes I mean something that someone really thinks about something very deeply. They *really* think about something.

The difference is something really hard to explain. It's a little flash of understanding that flashes in and then suddenly is gone but leaves a feeling of content.

May 17

I think that there are actually two types of dry spells.

The first type is of course the dry spell when you can't think of any ideas.

The second type is when kids just have a dry spell in writing. This kind of dry spell goes together with the thinking one. Kids just seem to get tired of writing journal entries.

To really try to get you to understand this idea I am going to explain how I got it.

Mr. Jacobs was saying that everyone in our class must have experienced at least once when a journal entry was exciting. Well there is this type of thing. But in between this time is a time when writing is literally a problem and a bore. Just an extra load on your mind. This is what I classify as the second type of dry spell. It's a period where you're all down and out as far as entries are concerned.

The reason I said this kind of dry spell goes with the thinking one is because the time when you feel, "All down and out" is the time when you can't think of an entry.

So the two dry spells go together. In fact, the more I think about it I've almost begun thinking that they're just one dry spell and I've specifically picked the two sides and see them merge together.

June 4

The best time to write a journal entry is when you have just gotten your idea and you're still very much excited by the idea.

There is only one problem in writing your entry at that time. That time is usually the most inconvenient time to write your journal idea.

The listener and/or reader may be thinking right now, "Why can't you just jot your idea down in note form and write it up later?"

That's a good thing to do when you are caught in that position and it is usually the answer to the problem. In fact that's what I used to do when I had the problem and then it solved it very easily.

But now I've found it to be very different when I run into this situation and use the solution I have in the past. The difference is that now it doesn't. It's a puzzling thing and very often it turns out alot of frustration (all from me).

It may be that I have entered a more sophisticated stage of journal writing and different things happen to me when I get involved in a new idea.

The way I would describe this happening is that now the only time I am really excited in an idea and can do a good job of writing it up is when I think the idea up. This is when I get the "flash" and after that the idea is no longer exciting.

P.S. This entry I feel explains why this is the first entry I've written in a rather long period of time. This I say because it is what has been happening to me ever since I started on the three system.*

---

*The three system was the system under which the kids could cut down to three entries a week if they promised that those entries would be of the highest quality.

Techniques and Problems of Running a Journal Program

A teacher, or anyone else for that matter, has a limited amount of time to devote to any one job. The journal program takes time. It takes time to read the children's entries, comment on them, make corrections, and check to see if the corrections are made. If you are really excited by their entries, it takes time because you start thinking about new ideas yourself. I found by having my children keep journals of new ideas I displaced other things I would normally do. The amount of time spent reading and enjoying journals is not much when added up on a weekly basis — probably four hours a week. But, being human, there are a limited number of things one can put one's best quality efforts into during the course of any one day or week. My observation and guess is that if the journals are not read regularly (at least once a week — twice a week would be better) the children lose interest. They like to have a constant reader and they like to have their very hard work acknowledged and appreciated. Don't we all? So if you plan to try such a program be prepared to displace other things. Not only will you displace things that you would do after the children leave school but you will also displace things that are done during the school day. This is because time needs to be taken to discuss the spirit and mechanics of journals all year long. Telling children about journals once at the begining of the year will not achieve results. I found in running this program that I went from an average of one composition a week to one every other or every third week. For the most part I dropped a formal spelling program and had the kids use the words they misspelled as their spelling words. There were other things that also got short shrift but you cannot fit the entire body of man's knowledge into the elementary school curriculum just because there are some who would like to try it. The best word I think of to describe this is "missingitis." We feel guilty because this one thing or that one thing or both are not being covered. Maybe some day a

33

way will be found to cram that entire body of knowledge into a child's head, but I would rather not be around to see it.

There are many problems connected with having the children keep journals. Basically you are asking kids to do something that for all of us is *the* most disagreeable task — to think. We would much rather do some job, any job, which doesn't require trying to get new ideas and organize nebulous thoughts into a coherent entity. How quickly we are prepared to take on a routine, mechanical activity which gives us the excuse of doing something useful and permits us to avoid the really important job. Children are not much different from adults in this. They would much prefer to be assigned a task which they can do without involving their minds. At first they respond to the journal by writing entries that are a log of their days' activities.

The first year I started journals these logs were my exclusive reading diet for September and October. Not being certain myself of what I could expect from the kids and what a good journal entry was, it was difficult for me to help them see in concrete terms what it was I was seeking. We had discussions about new ideas. I lectured, I encouraged, I bullied, and I praised things that showed the slightest spirit. Gradually the emphasis shifted from recording events to noting creative thought. Reading some of the more promising entries aloud seemed to stimulate the others. By January and February most of the children were occasionally writing very impressive things. Some were doing this regularly. Success seems to breed success and the children began to benefit from each other. In March I was asked to introduce the technique to another class of the same age and the results from that class in March were almost of the calibre my class was turning out then. First, I had a much clearer idea of what the journal was about and was able to read some of the more spectacular entries from my class to the new class and, second, the new group had the benefit of hearing about journals from my kids. Interestingly, the following year when I started the program with a new class, the calibre of thinking and writing in September was equal to the calibre in March of the previous year. I had learned and the kids had heard about journals from older friends and siblings.

Sandy Sher, who has used journals in her classes for three years, worked out a guide for introducing the journals. She describes this procedure which she has found successful:

> On the first day of school I presented my class with 11 open-ended questions to which they were to react, such as: What is an idea? When do you get ideas? How do certain ideas make you feel? What makes different people have different ideas?
>
> For the next two days we discussed their reactions to these questions. I tried to stress that there was no one right answer and that it was important for them to participate in the discussion since it would possibly make creative writing easier for them.
>
> In the meantime, for homework, I had asked them to write at least a half page on any topic that was on their minds. In the last discussion of

that week, I tried to have them connect what they had been saying about expressing ideas and thinking critically. Next, I asked them to read over what they had written and to determine for themselves whether their entries expressed complete ideas and how they might look deeper into those ideas.

It is apparent from some of the entries in Chapter IV that the children are well aware of the problem of producing journal entries regularly. Not only are they being asked to write daily but they are being asked to think, organize their thinking, re-think, and come up with something exciting. Out of last year's class of twenty-six, approximately ten children came up with something exciting to read at least once a week; another seven or eight, at least once every other week; another five, once a month; and the rest, about once every other month.

I was constantly torn between a series of conflicting motives while administering this program. If I pressured the kids too hard into producing five days a week, there was the danger of making their writing sterile. If I respected the difficulties inherent in trying to think and describe new ideas five days a week and told the children not to worry about doing it every single day, there would have been many who would not have produced at all. As a result, a series of compromises took place. If I felt that a child was sincere and doing his best, I would overlook a reasonable quantity of missed entries. In fact, my advice to all of them was not to try to make up missed entries, but to start from the present. Otherwise a child might have ten or fifteen entries to do at once. This certainly defeats the purpose of this technique as it results in writing for the sake of writing rather than for the sake of thinking.

The requirement of five days a week was five days out of seven and any five days could be chosen. In practice, what happened toward the end of the year was that many children averaged three entries a week. Roughly a third did this and another third averaged less than three a week. What I did toward the end of the second year was to have those children who chose to, make a contract with me whereby they would promise their best quality thinking three times a week instead of five. This was actually a recognition of reality because, except for the very conscientious, many were already doing only three a week. In addition, if they wrote an entry covering several pages, they were permitted to count it as several entries.

Something that many children found useful in overcoming sterile periods was to make brief notes, either in their journals or someplace else, of the new ideas or questions they thought of. Some of them got quite good at stashing away ideas for future use and some managed to hoard quite a few. When they did that they felt quite wealthy. Wouldn't you if you had lots of good new ideas ready to be trotted out at a moment's notice?

Another problem of considerable delicacy was how to comment about each entry a child wrote. After all, the children are being asked to put forth the best that their minds can produce which puts their inner selves on the line. Sometimes the subject itself is very personal to them whether or not it seems that way to the reader of the journal. Most people seem to do better work with praise than with damning and children are no exception. Furthermore, can you give your best quality thinking and creative effort when you know all you will get will be criticism or indifference? Yet, how can you praise a description of the day's happenings when the child is being asked to come up with profound thinking? Usually, if an entry was somewhat close to getting the point I would say so in positive terms. I would tell a child that the idea he had described in that day's entry was terrific and it needed more explanation to make it even more fascinating. I would suggest that he continue that day's entry another day. This had the advantages of not penalizing him, not making the process unpleasant, and relieving him of the worry of having to come up with a new idea for another day. It helped many children grasp the idea of completeness of an entry.

The following series of entries illustrates how this technique worked with one boy:

Harry: July 16
I am helping my sister on the recorder. She is 7 years old and she is doing very well. She is on page 2 of *Enjoy Your Recorder*. She practices every day.

I commented in his journal, "What's your new idea here?" and I also suggested to him that he go on with this subject in his next day's entry.

Harry: July 18
The reason I thought this new and exciting was because I have never taught anyone in music. I have helped her a lot. She never had anything with music before.

My written comment was, "Much better!" When I spoke to him in positive terms I suggested that he might want to go even further by explaining why he felt it was new and exciting. This he did.

Harry: July 19
I feel that teaching is very exciting. I work with my sister. I get the feeling that teaching her is fun as long as she listens.

My written comment, "You've got me terribly excited. Please keep going."

Harry: July 22
The reason I'll teach her only she listens is because it gives me more confidence. When I have confidence I feel like I want to keep on. I'll work better.

My written comment was, "Great!" and I said nothing to him about continuing. He went on on this subject.

Harry: July 23
    I think as long as I think about teaching, I'll want to do it more. The
more I want to teach I have more fun.
    When I get older I'll learn more and be able to teach other brothers and
sisters. I think as long as I teach I'll learn things just as the person or
people I'm teaching learn.

                         July 24
    I learn when I teach because she knows things I don't know when I
teach her things where she knows things. She brings those things out. I do
this on other things and learn more.

"GREAT! Keep it up." was my comment.

Harry: July 26
    I don't only learn by being taught and getting things by teaching. I
learn when I teach by having to look up things. I get the information and
think about it. I get ideas think about them, look to see if my ideas are
correct.

When I made my comment in Harry's July 16th entry and commented to him
about the other entries I felt that he was ready for pushing and that he would
respond well. Sometimes, if I felt the child understood what he should have been
doing, I just commented, "New ideas?" How far you push a child in this situation is a matter of judgement. Until you are sure of yourself with a child, it is
better to err on the side of not pushing.

The results of praise are very gratifying as is shown by Natalie's entry. You
can see the dramatic effect my comment had on her in her second journal entry
during the summer session.

Natalie: July 8
    I covered my whole paper white and left some blank spaces. The paper
was white. I then painted the blank spaces blue. I thought this would look
good. It did. But I was too proud of it and painted big thick black lines
down it. Then red spots. It did not look good. That goes to show do not
get carryed away.

                         July 9
    Yesterday I wrote a journal. I knew it was wrong. I was sure it was
wrong. When the teacher gave the journal back to me it said, "Terrific!"
Now I know it does not hurt to try things.

Perhaps the quality of the following entries also reflects the effect of the
initial praise.

Natalie: July 15
    I have a friend. She is my best friend but if she disagrees with some-
thing she says it. Like when she does not like my dress she says, "I don't

like your dress, I like plain colors." She says things like that. But if I do that she will get mad at me. I do like her. But if she did not do that I would like her even more. I learned from that if you keep things to yourself you will have more friends and more people will like you.

August 1

How does a baby's mind work? It may be like our minds. I think a baby's mind works almost like ours. I wonder what they think about. I do not think a baby thinks like us about. But again they may. When they eat or see something they want to eat it. If they do not like the taste they have sense not to eat it. I think some babies have a smart mind.

Eventually many of my comments became fairly stereotyped much as I tried to avoid it. Either there would be no comment or "good," "very good," "excellent," "terrific," or "great." I explained to the children that the lack of comment on an entry did not have a particular significance and that a positive comment did not mean I agreed with the subject matter of the entry. A valiant attempt was made to have the children see that it did not matter what my evaluation was. Their own evaluation of their work was much more significant than mine. I explained to them that they knew themselves and their work much better than I did because they lived with themselves twenty-four hours a day while my personal contact with them was in the order of a few minutes a day. There were some very interesting results from this approach. One was that the children felt free to discuss and argue their report card grades with me and this was encouraged. The other was that some journal entries were written about my comments about their journals.

Craig: May 24

There is one thing I have to say about journals. It is that some ideas are not interesting to you but they might be to another person. What I am trying to get at is that you or anyone else cannot make good or bad or very good or excellent about a person's entry.

Obviously this is an extremely important point. Many times I found myself indifferent to an entry until I reread it and on second reading managed to see the excitement of that entry to the writer.

Another internal conflict of mine was whether to mark mistakes of spelling, grammar, and sentence construction. How does one do this (and for some children there are a large number of mistakes) without getting so wrapped up in correcting and avoiding mistakes that you and the children lose sight of the importance of thinking?

What happened was another compromise. I put a vertical line in the margin which meant there was a mistake of some kind on that line. When the children got back their journals they were expected to find the mistakes and correct them. If I made two parallel vertical lines in the margin, the child knew that was a section I thought was particularly good. When all corrections had been made up to a point the child put a paper clip on that page. Then both he and I knew where to start the next time.

If I thought the child needed an explanation of what was wrong, I wrote, "see me." He was welcome to do that in any case. Sometimes, if the mistake was one that might have been too sophisticated for me to explain to him, I just went ahead and corrected it myself. Sometimes I made the correction because it seemed that the child was becoming too burdened with corrections and losing sight of the importance of thinking.

When I develop standards for journal writing and other classroom work at the beginning of every year, I stress that copying over is a waste of time. My request to the children is to write the entry neatly the first time, perhaps on the basis of notes, but not to plan on copying over. If there are mistakes, then a neat erasure or crossout, an insertion, and whatever else is needed to correct the material should be used. If there is need for a drastic reorganization, then there is a purpose for copying over. The mind is not engaged when copying over. The children's time is too valuable to waste on the process and I have found that the result of copying over is frequently that the mistakes in the original are still there — plus some new ones. Many of the ten to twelve year olds I teach take the first opportunity they can to copy over. It is an activity involving no thinking and no real work. They delight in it until they learn that it is one of my little prejudices. What it really does is to interfere with thinking.

It is important not to let the mechanics get in the way of the main idea. Bert Lloyd, one of the other teachers who has been using the journal techniques, does not mark the journals for mistakes at all. He feels that the less structure imposed on the students, the more likely they are to be creative. If I could eradicate enough of the Puritan in me, I would follow suit. (I did just this when I was a demonstration teacher this summer. I did not correct any entries and the resulting quality of thought, spelling, and grammar was at least equal to, if not superior to, what my previous classes did.) Bert makes an analogy: "I recalled my old baseball days in little league — had the coaches lectured at us for a number of years as to the characteristics that could make a good hitter, runner, and fielder, I daresay none of us would ever have been able to catch a ball."

What do you do with an entry that is obviously incorrect? Here, for instance, Bill has made an observation that shows perception and thought but he is absolutely wrong:

Bill: September 20
I wonder how the men who make the maps know exactly how the land is. They could look at it but lots of maps cover large areas. Even in planes you can't see an area as big as the whole city of Washington, D.C.

Do you tell him he is wrong but that his thinking is excellent? Do you just comment on how good his thinking is and let him find out for himself that he is wrong? My strong inclination is to follow the latter course. He is now sensitive to the problem and will make the connection himself when he has the opportunity. It will be much more effective learning for him. It will not discourage him from developing other ideas because he is afraid of disapproval or is used to having many of his ideas called wrong. Several of the series of entries in the physical phenomena section show clearly that children do make new observations and change their minds about the conclusions they have made.

Sometimes the comments of teachers cut off the children's thinking and have the active effect of discouraging the free ranging of the mind. The two entries below with the teacher's comments show this.

Ilse: June 2
We were talking about the human body. We conversed about respiration and found out that on one or two times people were saved after being underwater for fifteen or twenty minutes. These people must have something in their body that saved them. Some people would call this a miracle but I don't believe in miracles. I wonder what saved these people.

"I think what saved the person, Ilse, was the rescuer who wanted them to live."

Ilse: May 16
Many times I wonder why I get red when I cry. On board ship I swam in a swimming pool of salt water. When I came out my face wasn't red. I thought at first maybe the salt in my tears made my face red. But it doesn't. Why do peoples faces get red when they cry?

"It probably has to do with emotions and the blood rushing to your face when you cry."

There is a great temptation to answer the questions the kids raise. However, the answers do not serve to promote more thinking and observation.

Handling the entry which screams at you that it is wrong presents another problem. But, even with entries which seem wrong to you, you should be very sparing and reserved in the comments you make and reluctant to make a comment at all.

Ceceile: February 7
I wonder why the Jewish people don't believe in Jesus. They were the one's who killed Jesus but still they don't believe in Jesus.
There's another religion that doesn't believe in God. I wonder why. Don't they know that God made them. If it wasn't for God, nothing would be created.

Obviously there is some confusion in her mind on several things. The temptation to set her right was strong but I resisted it.

The importance of being on guard against setting a child straight in this context cannot be over emphasized. Children are bound to hit areas of high emotional impact for us as Cecile did for me in this entry and Bill did in the entry on page 42. Your first reaction is to want to say something to the child on the pretext of teaching, but your emotions are so highly charged in this situation that you are likely to achieve just the opposite effect of what you want.

Many of the children express concern for God and for religion in their entries and pose some very difficult questions. The question raised below has been raised again and again in different forms in entries by many children.

Thelma: May 31
    Today we saw a movie on the Middle Ages.
    How, if the Christian religion is against fighting, did they justify going plundering the countryside and butchering the people?
    I intend to find out.

She spent a good deal of time working on that question and as far as I recall never resolved it to her satisfaction. Have you? Is it a question that should be resolved? We need to refrain from answering religious questions as well as questions raised about physical phenomena, interpersonal relationships, etc. Not only are we stopping the child's thinking if we answer, but we may well be wrong. Certainly this is just as true of a moral or religious question as it is of a question about physical phenomena. After all, our scientific knowledge changes with an ever increasing rapidity. I am not saying the children's questions should never be answered. What I am saying is that, in the context of journals and creative thinking, the questions they raise should rarely be answered.

What happens when the child describes actions of his that you deplore? The following entry by Teresa illustrates this:

Theresa: March 7
    Today I was wondering why when you pinch somebody that when you take a whole bunch it doesn't hurt but when you hardly take any skin it hurts. I did this to my baby brother today and took a big piece of his arm and pinched it. Then I took a little piece of his arm and pinched it. By the way he reacted it seemed that when I pinched the little piece of his arm it hurt more than when I pinched the big piece of his arm. Is it because when you pinch a great big part you can only feel it where your fingers are and when you pinch a little section you can feel it all over because the space is little? What do you think?

In this entry Theresa has made some excellent observations and done some verification of them. She has shown some perceptive thinking. My reaction to this was to speak to her privately and tell her that I thought the entry was an excellent one while I deplored her experimentation. Theresa is a consistently good thinker and journal writer. I am sure my remarks did not stultify her. When I made them I tried to make them with good feeling behind the words. Obviously you have to use your judgement in dealing with such a situation.

If the children feel truly free to allow their minds and pens to range freely in the area of new ideas they are bound to come up with entries that are quite critical of their teacher. The entry below is a case in point.

Bill: February 10

Today in class a girl said something about positive and negative on a battery. Mr. Jacobs replied by saying, "How can you tell the difference between positive and negative?" Not a person in the class knew. So he told us to think about it. Teachers always do this. Why? Whatever anybody says they find a flaw in it or say investigate more or something like that. Whenever you make an oral report to the class they mess it up by finding every pinhole they can in it. Teachers often say this is true of students, however, I find this is only true because teachers criticize them so much they just can't wait to give it back to the teachers. I think this whole problem could be solved if teachers would only quit criticizing their kids so much.

Bill has hit where it really hurts. I have prided myself on my positive attitude when commenting to children. Good teachers have always tried to turn questions back to children and ask them what they think, how they can find out, or any one of a thousand variations of this. They feel that it is important to develop children's thinking in everything done in the classroom and that this is a useful technique. I have felt pride in doing this kind of thing and along comes Bill with his rather unpleasant remarks about it. My first reaction was, "That ungrateful, narrow-minded little wretch." However, when I stopped to think carefully about what he had said, I realized that there was a lot to it. Perhaps these techniques were being overused. As teachers, we can not see the unpleasant ramifications of many of the things we take pride in and frequently are unaware of most of the effects that they have on children.

Bill's entry is certainly a good example of what we tell children to do when we say to them, "It's all right to disagree but do it politely." Once I got over my feelings of anger at Bill I was able to realize that he had done just that and some very profound thinking as well. I was then able to talk to him privately and ask him if I could project the entry for the whole class to read as long as I kept the author anonymous. He agreed and when we talked about his entry there was a most lively discussion in the class. Some felt very strongly that Bill had grossly misstated the situation and others saw his point and agreed with it. Everyone seemed to feel that it was an excellent entry.

This brings up another problem about dealing with journals—that of anonymity. The children, when they are trying hard, put themselves on the line. For children who are in the fifth and sixth grades this is difficult. Frequently it is their innermost thoughts they are describing. I can remember having many of the same feelings as a child and would never have dreamed of writing them down. Even when the journal writer is describing his wonderings about physical phenomena he is revealing himself. For this reason it is important that the children have anonymity and the strong feeling that their entries will not be read without their permission. Even that is tricky because it is hard for a child to say no to a request from a teacher. This book itself is a violation of the point I am making.

I also referred to projecting entries on the overhead projector. After this was done several times, some of the children commented that they felt that it was wrong and were bothered by it. My purpose had been to give them a chance to see and discuss a wide variety of entries of differing quality and approach. I will not do it again. Rather, to avoid embarrassing the authors, I will use the entries that I have already collected from previous classes. In some cases, children will truly volunteer entries and these can be capitalized on. For instance, when I asked my children if any of them wanted to choose some of their best writing for submission to the school magazine, some of them submitted journal entries.

Sometimes children told me or wrote in their journals that they did not want an entry read aloud or they did not want anyone else to read it. I respected these requests and encouraged the children to do this in order to have them feel freer in what they wrote.

When I saw the parents of my class as a group or individually, I suggested to them that their children's journals should be read only with the kids' permission. I also strongly suggested that they not put pressure on the kids to come up with *correct* ideas. Occasionally a parent and I would agree that some pressure should be applied to the child to get him to make his entries and correct his mistakes. This did not happen very often. In many cases, the parents made routine inquiries of their children about the completion of their homework which is enough of a reminder to a child that his parent cares about what he is doing. A teacher using the journals of new ideas in another community found that she had to spell these things out loudly and clearly for the parents of her students because they interfered with their children's journals to a large extent.

That same teacher also found that her children were so enthusiastic about getting new ideas and writting journal entries that she had them writing two entries a day. Many times they were permitted to write them in school when the idea occurred to them. My class frequently had opportunities to write entries in school. This was a profitable way for those children who finished other jobs sooner than the rest to employ the time of waiting for the others.

In the course of collecting journal entries for this book, I kept a master journal. If an entry was one that I thought would be useful, I put an "MJ" on the page which was a request to the child to copy it over for my journal. The master journals were read by many of the children but this did not seem to bother the authors nearly so much as the public discussions. Another effect of the master journal was that it unintentionally became a gold star system. Much as I tried to point out that there were many excellent entries I had not "MJ"ed because I could not use them, it became a matter of prestige and comparative counting. This gold star system did not turn out to be all bad as it stimulated the kids to read what others had written in the master journal as well as to write on a higher level. It is not something that I would recommend unqualifiedly. I started collecting entries because I thought some of them were so great that I could not bear to part with them when the children kept their journals at the end of the year. I did not want to keep the journals themselves because I definitely felt that they belonged to the children.

At Page School we take our sixth graders into the mountains for a week of outdoor education. (See footnote, p. 9.) The stress is on studying those things out of doors that cannot be studied indoors. We do not teach camping skills or go in much for physical education while we are there because we feel that parents can provide the camping skills and the children will get enough physical activity while active in the academic areas. We have been hard put to find a vehicle to help tie the children's experiences together. In desperation we used the journals and asked the children to make journal entries about the new ideas they got from their outdoor education each day. It worked to some extent. Some of the entries from that week have been quoted. However, the more vocal and abler journal writers complained bitterly that being assigned to find new ideas on a specific subject was not compatible with the spirit of journals of new ideas. They were right. What we were doing to them was trying to make sure they were getting something out of the experience, putting the last little bit in to make sure they were working, and generally being fussy, hovering bosses. I often wonder why it is that there are so many things we do that satisfy our adult needs rather than the children's needs. Of course, when we do them we say that we are meeting the children's needs.

There are some schools that used the journal techniques just for the outdoor education week and in that context it is probably not much of a violation of the spirit. Here are two excellent entries from one of these schools.

Carolyn: November 7
    I enjoyed the trip to Harper's Ferry very much, but I wondered how the historians and archaelogists started out to get their information they aren't assigned to look up.

Yvonne: November 7
    I wonder how the archaelogists knew where to dig for the relics. They always seem to dig at just the right place. I also wonder how historians can figure what kind of stone a building was or what a certain field was used for. I just can't figure out how they knew about the hogs.

There is also the problem of the completeness of an entry. This is a most critical problem and one of the most difficult to deal with. I have stressed to the children that the entry should be complete, which might require anything from a few sentences to a few pages. Obviously this leaves much room for a child to navigate within. Children, being just as anxious as the rest of us to avoid work, sometimes come up with remarkably short entries. Some of them are complete, but many are not. Some are good entries, but many are not. A technique that seemed to help this situation considerably was the projection of some of the very short, incomplete entries. The discussions were not on length but on completeness. Many were disturbed that an interesting question had been raised in a projected entry but that not enough information had been given. They expressed the feeling that they had been shown a teaser and wanted more.

Bernard:
Last year when I was watching my dad shoot a gun every time he shot the gun it jerked back. I wondered what caused it to do that.

Nancy: February
Today when I was eating a pear I noticed that something formed on the pear. I asked my mother about the pear. She said I sat the pear down and the air formed on the pear.

These are obviously incomplete. How do you develop standards of completeness when specifying length does not guarantee it and the demand for completeness leaves itself open to exploitation by children? For many children it is a long, slow process to learn how to write a complete journal entry and it is not unlike the kinds of things we ask of them in other areas. As the children catch the spirit of journal thinking and writing, their entries get longer. At the end of the year many of them average entries twice as long as their beginning of the year entries. However, it is important that we do not stress length or even make the kids feel guilty about short entries when the purpose is completeness. It is this spirit which is so important for them to come to feel.

VI

Conveying the Spirit of New Ideas

First, let me re-emphasize that this vehicle for stimulating children's thinking is one that should be used only by those who feel it does this and by those who get genuine enjoyment from it. If, as a teacher, you do not get a great deal of pleasure from this form, then drop it. If you do not anticipate getting pleasure from it, do not start to use it. If it is done because someone else thinks it should be done, the children are being put in a position where they are being asked to please someone rather than express themselves. If it is being done because of pressures that have nothing to do with its purposes, things are going to be said and done to the children that will not allow them to range freely over a host of subjects and the results are likely to be neat, accurate essays or descriptions of events, and totally meaningless because they will not involve real thinking. There are other forms for encouraging children to think creatively and each one has to find those methods which suit him best. Preferably they will be methods from which we will derive enjoyment. If not, there will be little joy and less learning for the children in them. If you are terribly worried about every mistake being corrected, about not having inaccuracies in a journal, about neatness, etc., don't use the journal to have the children conform to these things.

The most important thing that will convey the spirit of this kind of thinking to the children is your own enjoyment of their thinking. You do not have to gush for them to get the message. In fact, false gushing is a good way to give children the idea that you do not believe in what you are doing.

The spirit is one of constantly observing, inquiring, ruminating, hypothesizing, re-observing, and re-inquiring. The subject matter is everything in the world and some things not in it. The spirit is one that in the ideal becomes a system of constant self-teaching. Many of my children have told me that they plan to keep writing journals after they leave my class. This is particularly true of those who have gotten a great deal of satisfaction from the process. My reply to them has been, "Fine, but the habit of thinking is much more important. If it comes to a choice between writing and thinking, forget the writing and do the thinking."

As I mentioned earlier, the first time I introduced this idea of writing new ideas to a class (sixth grade) there was a long hard pull to get the kind of thinking that came more easily later. However, when I introduced the technique to someone else's class that same year they caught on immediately. This had nothing to do with the way the children were grouped. Both groups were heterogeneously arranged as was the combination fifth-sixth grade class I worked with the second year. Most of my second year's class also caught on immediately. In addition, I substituted one morning in a third grade class and tried to get them to catch this spirit of writing on a one-shot basis. All of these attempts were successful sooner than was the first try. Several factors were particularly important in this. One was that I am sure the children felt my very strong commitment to new ideas and this form of work. (Children are gifted at observing what is really important to their teachers. As John Holt says, this is how they survive. Their survival depends on their doing this for a new boss each year.) They also felt much greater clarity of purpose on my part.

Another factor that helped was reading aloud inspiring and interesting entries of other children. Doing this gave them something to visualize. When I talked to them about writing up their new ideas, questions, and excitements, I am sure it did not mean nearly so much to them as hearing how other kids had done it.

Some reacted by saying, "They used all the new ideas." I have a feeling that this reaction means that the child has really become excited about what he has heard because he identifies in the entries things that he has observed and felt. A child at this point is not yet in the habit of being constantly on the lookout for new and exciting things to describe in his journal. Once he has found a few things for himself the possibilities become broader and broader. Overcoming the reluctance of an older child to show his excitement to a teacher is part of the difficulty. By the time a child gets to the fifth and sixth grade he is considerably less spontaneous and open than he was in the early grades. A big difficulty in getting the child started is overcoming his reluctance to reveal his inner feelings. This takes time and it takes integrity on the part of the teacher. The teacher has to be someone whom the child can trust. It is particularly difficult since he has recently and painfully learned how to avoid doing this. Why and how we as teachers, and society in general, teach him to stop being spontaneous and open should be the subject of a great deal of earnest speculation and research on our part. In any case, our problem is to bring the ingenuousness of the younger child back to life in a more sophisticated form.

Once again, a genuine enthusiasm for their enthusiasm, their questions, and their new ideas will go a long way toward getting children to do profound thinking. If you get real pleasure from thinking about the puzzles of the world around you and enjoy trying to solve them, this attitude of pleasure and curiosity will be communicated to the children.

As this past year progressed, I found myself writing journal entries. I was caught up in the enthusiasm of new ideas. These entries were projected for the children to read and criticize. Sometimes while discussing the entries, I told the children I had written them. Our discussions were in terms of, "Do you think the author meant this?" "Don't you think the author could have carried this part further?" They were as ruthless in discussing the clarity and completeness of my entries as they had been with each other's. The children took pleasure from my writing of journal entries and would complain that I was not doing it as often as they were required to do.

Another way of stimulating the children is to have them work together. In one case we asked the children from my class and another class to write a description of how a journal of new ideas works for someone who had never done it. We then paired the children for a thirty-minute discussion in which they were to come up with recommendations for good journal writing for all of us. The reports included journal entries they felt were illustrative of the spirit. It seemed to work well. Kids learning from kids is a very effective teaching technique.

Bonnie: April 21
Why is it that when kids teach a subject in class it is less confusing than if a teacher taught it? I think that a child who has gone through an experience in which something was confusing would know how and where it was confusing and then be able to teach it with less confusion. I am going to cite such an example.

We are doing map skills, and a lot of the time when Mr. Jacobs tells us directions kids get lost. I think if one of these kids taught the subject they may be able to teach kids and have them less confused. The reason I say this is that the child that is teaching will have had the experience of being confused and able to avoid more confusion.

On the other hand like Mr. Jacobs says, "Confusion is the beginning of learning." In this case the kids would get confused and by continuously getting confused and then finding out their mistakes they would probably learn better.

Bonnie is a smart kid. She hedges her bets. She, like so many of the rest of us, is plagued with seeing many sides of a problem. Her first point is a good one even though it strikes close to home. Teaching map skills is one of those areas where I feel I do my best job as a teacher. I know the area well and maps are an avocation of mine. I think I have analyzed the problems kids have in learning to read maps and have managed to break down these problems so that kids come up with a good understanding of them. Poor Bonnie probably had some idea she was treading on a most sensitive toe and so she straddled the fence. My first reaction to this entry was that she was right about kids teaching kids but not about map reading. "I can do it better." It is this feeling we have that gets in our way. Sure, I know maps better but can I teach the skills to kids better? What would happen if I let them go a bit?

Many of us are distressed by letting our children learn on their own, with other children, or in ways that are not teacher-directed. Children working on projects of their own devising is an example of this. We keep feeling that we should be doing something more. We do not want some child to miss what goes on in the room. We feel that if we are not participating more directly, either through leading a discussion, a question and answer period, directed reading, etc. that the children might not be learning. Why we feel this way opens up a Pandora's box of possibilities. However, we are torn and go only part way toward the ideals set forth by the world's great educators and reiterated in education courses.

The thought that recurs to me is that I keep getting in the way of my children's learning. How can I get out of the way and still feel I am teaching? Occasionally I become jubilant because I find that when I have let go, my children have actually learned a great deal. However, I keep forgetting that much of their learning is undetected by me. We need to become more conscious of what learning is and how we can observe it.

What all of us who are responsible for the education of children, and this includes parents, need to do is to find some new meaningful roles for ourselves. These roles will differ from our present view of what teaching is. Teachers will be doing a number of things such as acting as learning counselors, resource people, and administrators of the varied activities taking place rather than lecturing, drilling, or questioning children. When classrooms become like this we will recognize in an appropriate way that very little learning to think occurs because a teacher teaches something and the child learns it.

Excellence in thinking as reflected in the journal entries does not necessarily relate to previous academic achievement. Many highly creative entries have come from kids who do not do well in school work. I have noticed a good many children whose general academic performance has improved considerably during the course of a year writing journal entries. I suspect this has a lot to do with the children getting the feeling that the output of their minds is of considerable worth. When they get to feeling this way they are feeling much more confident of themselves and, as success breeds success, their other work improves.

If children are interested in their work they will learn better. Over the years I have been searching for techniques to use which would get children more interested and involved in their work. The journals of new ideas have provided the children with a way of getting thoroughly involved in things that interest them and because of this they have been thinking better and more profoundly. Keeping a journal also has the advantage of being able to achieve these results with less of the usual bullying of children to get the work done.

Another thing I have noticed but not measured is that many children who have had difficulties with reading and writing skills seem to have improved considerably with this program. I must emphasize that these are personal observations and not measured results.

Bert Lloyd describes his experiences with such a child:

A youngster in my sixth grade class had been tested and found to have a very low intelligence quotient. He was also functioning on about a first grade verbal level. He read very poorly, his spelling was almost undiscernible, and his conception of a sentence was nil. However, I did notice that when it came to creative writing, his ideas were on a par with the sharpest child in the class. For example: How do rain droplets form? Why does the white of an egg spread out and the yellow does not? How is it that boys and girls both have rather unique characteristics that contribute to our culture?

The interesting thing that happened after several weeks of journal writing was that the other children began to respect him deeply for his ability to produce superior journal entries.

Sandy Sher developed an evaluation paper to help the children in her class analyze their own journal work. It was intended to help them see their year's work and to decide whether such an exercise was of value to them personally. It was an important part of the process of enabling the children to carry away a feeling that the journals had meaning for them.

This book is not a report on research. Rather it is the result of my searches for ways to develop children's thinking. I have noticed great improvement in the thinking and writing of children as a result of the journal program but these are subjective observations. I hope there will come a time when we will have the tools to measure changes in children's behavior more precisely and will be able to describe more accurately what are the most effective methods of learning. In the meantime, we must use the research we have and make educated guesses as to the best methods.

I have been told that children cannot develop their thinking unless they have something specific to think about. It is said that problems have to be organized and the appropriate level for the child has to be found. My experience leads me to believe that children can certainly develop their thinking without this kind of external help. The essential ingredient is that a concern for a child's thinking be expressed in such a way that the child feels the concern and is given the opportunity to think in more than narrow channels. The problem approach to developing thinking may work well, but I think that it restricts the range of ideas and the chances of making connections in fields other than the one in which the problem is set.

My children have written brilliant things in their journals. They have written things that keep me on the edge of my seat when reading them. At times their writings have made my day and given me a bounce for a few days that has made me feel that what we are doing together is fantastically worthwhile. But there are other ways of doing the same job. I felt the same way many times before I ever introduced journals of new ideas to my kids. The children's profound thinking has come during many activities including physical education, writing, discussions, private talks, chess and gō games. If we take a true joy in breakthroughs that we and they make in thinking, the method doesn't matter. They will get the message and so will we.

VII

Random Thoughts and Quotations from Children's Journals

These last remarks are afterthoughts. I remember my father saying to me, "Think," when I was faced with a problem. When the word is used in this way, the user really means, "You're not working hard enough. If only you would just sweat a little more and have pain you could solve your problems." These people are talking about something I have never understood. My reaction to the command has always been guilt because maybe I was not doing enough, and fear that even if I worked harder I would not succeed. That reaction has really gotten in the way of doing productive and creative thinking.

What we need to do is to disassociate work from pain. Creative thinking does not have to be painful or unpleasant. While it is being done it is very demanding and it is hard work. But why do we insist upon looking at hard work as something that cannot be pleasurable? I guess what I am trying to say is that if you are going to try some of the methods that I have described do not put the emphasis on the pain. Do not tell the children to think in such a way that the message they are getting is "work harder and get more pain from it." On the other hand, there is no need to pretend that thinking and writing up new ideas are easy.

Something that has never ceased to amaze me in my reading of journal entries is the uncanny ability of children to describe things so well. There are many interesting and subtle experiences we all have while on our passage through this world and some of them are very hard to describe in words. Many children have done this job and done it superlatively.

The most difficult chore in preparing this book was choosing the children's entries. It was hard to know if I was choosing an entry because it was good or because it showed the best effort of a particular child. It was also difficult because I wanted entries that illustrated the points being made and so many entries did. I am devoting most of this section to children's entries which are not being used to illustrate anything except the quality of thinking that kids can do.

Michelle: October 25
Since the mathematicians get new ideas on new math I got one right now. Since the radius is half of the diameter so I got an idea on the half of the radius. I call it the riameter from the radius and the diameter. Since the radius makes the diameter one-half so the riameter makes the diameter one-fourth.

Gladys: October 20
Yesterday I was helping my mother with housework. She told me to wash the windows. I looked in the cabinet, but we didn't have any windex, so I found a rag put water in it and began washing. My mother caught me and told me to put some spic and span in it so I did. All of a sudden the dirt started wearing away on the towel. I thought, "If the dirt of the window is on the towel, how can the window be getting clean?" How can it because the dirt was on the towel and it was getting clearer? Did the spic and span eat up the dirt? But that couldn't be true because one time I was washing the window and it was still getting clean.

Donald: December 14
I'm going to tell you something you've never heard in a journal before, nothing! That's right nothing. I think of nothing a lot of times. I wonder why I think of nothing. Why, with all the things to think about all I can think of is nothing. But if I say I'm thinking of nothing I mean I'm not thinking. But I'm really thinking of something I'm thinking of nothing. This is like Mr. Lloyd's useful and useless kick. Just think in this page all said is nothing.

Faye: January 20
When we finished the Alice in Wonderland play, I realized that it went so well because everyone did his part. If even a few people had goofed off, the play would have been ruined for the most part. It reminds me of the conjunctive property. No matter how many true parts there are in a statement, it only takes one false part to make the statement false.

Tina: February 6
What is love? To me love is a feeling that you have to have. It is when you feel lonesome and when you are just to yourself. When you are at the age of 11 or 13. I think that it would be hard to understand what the meaning of it is. When you get married you have a feeling of what it is like. When you have a boyfriend you are just beginning to know how you think of how it really started.

Marvin: April 28
I think adults are foolish at times too. For example, one day I was putting my gocart together and I pounded the nail in crooked. Well my dad got mad and told me about how simple it is to pound a nail in.
About ten minutes passed and my dad took the hammer from me and tried to pound the nail in. He tried twice and both times he bent it. After that he told me he was sorry and went inside.

Beverly: January 24
   Reading is fun I think. When you are reading your mind is stimulating. If you were reading a book and you thought that it was interesting you would finish it in a hurry. But if you didn't think that it was interesting you should not read it because you wouldn't get anything important out of it and your mind would not be stimulating. That is why you should always read a book that you like.

Michelle: December 10
   Sometimes when I read Dad's book of Shakespeare's plays, I wonder how he can write in that "flowery" language.
   Later I guessed that he picked up the idea from the Bible and how it is written.

Faye: December 1
   Earlier, I said that in space there is no such thing as direction. Now I was thinking that there is. If scientists are able to make a map of the moon or of all the planets together, wouldn't it be necessary to have directions on the maps to help locate or name certain locations? It's that way with a country on Earth when mapped. Why can't it be that way with space? In the future space likely will be a super-highway(s). To map these highways we would need directions.

Daphne: December 5
   Do you ever get the feeling when you have an old friend over for a few days and you talk about things you did with her or she around four years ago they are still funny for awhile but later on after you talk about it so much all of the fun and laughter kind of wears out?

Donald: March 21
   If there are people out there flying saucers they'd have to be tremendously more advanced than us to get here in the first place. I think I know why they don't show themselves. Just like us when men first came over here. We were more advanced than the Indians. Did we help them? No, we had as little to do with him as possible except to trade with him we always got the best out of the deal. We regarded the indian as too primitive to bother with. They couldn't compare with us. We cheated them out of their land.
   Well I think this is why they don't show themselves. They think us too "primitive" to bother with. They may one day cheat us out of Earth. You can't blame them you know.

Stephanie: Febraury 6
   When you get married and your sister becomes a relative to your wife's sister, shouldn't your mother become a relative to your wife's or husband's mother? I think that your mother or father should become a sister-in-law to your wife's mother. I think this because if your son or daughter gets married you should become well acquainted with his parents, in fact, you should become related.

Laura: October 19
   Today I was thinking why people get stuffed up noses. Last night I

woke up once with a stuffed up nose. I think that my problem is that I usually sleep with two pillows and last night I only slept with one pillow and so I was lower. But I wonder why other people get stuffed up noses. Maybe if you have a cold all the stuff in your nose goes out one nostril and into the other and so one nostril would have everything in it and the other nothing in it. Then one nostril would be clogged. Whenever I have a stuffed up nose I always feel awful and that I'm locked inside a room and I can't get out. Now I can imagine how people who are deaf, blind or mute must feel. They're all locked up inside a door and they have a lot of tantrums because they are desperate to get out of this locked door. I know that whenever I don't feel good I'm always grouchy and I get mad at everyone.

Marianne: October 27
    I wonder who invented sarcasm and why? Because it seems pretty much like a waste of time to me.

Ginger: November 15
    This is something I have wondered about for a long time. When a person dies do they continue their life, sort of, in heaven? Do they have any thoughts in their minds or do they just not think at all? That is a reason why I am not going to be all that disappointed and sad when I die because I will know what dead people think or if they think at all.

Grace: November 29
    If the river that ran through the German town of Hamlin in the Pied Piper's time was polluted, then I know why. It was the Pied Piper himself! If he got all the rats to jump in the river, and if there were as many rats as it's told, the bodies of the dead rats surely would have polluted the river. True? I think so.

Lawrence: December 6
    We can hear music and it gives us feelings, but why can't we touch it? We feel air blowing from an instrument. Is it considered feeling music?

Doris: December 8
    I know that in Africa people have dark skin because it's hot there and their skin protects them. But if their children are born here they have dark skin because of heredity. But if they keep having children will their skin keep getting lighter because they're living here?

Gloria: December 12
    If you weren't born the world would be a little different. There might not even be a war in Viet Nam now because every little thing you do sets off a chain reaction of little events. So really as small and unimportant as you may seem, you still have a little influence on history because if you hadn't done what you just did (reading this) you wouldn't have triggered off a chain of events and done what you're doing now.

Clarke: December 15
    I was looking through my journal when I noticed about the Dec. 8 entry about the older people getting shorter and then I mentioned it again

on Dec. 14 and said that their bones shrink. If this happens they wouldn't be able to move as easy as before. Is that why some old people can't do certain things that would seem easy to us?

Lisa: December 16
    When you read a book you sort of read the words as you would aloud except you read them silently. This is hard to put into words but why does it seem like you're talking aloud when you're really talking to yourself? What I mean is it seems as though you're talking aloud. Why can't you just think of the words without reading them? I've often read without thinking about this but just now I wondered about this and why my thoughts about reading are so difficult to put into words in a way that they can be understood.

                                                                     December 21
    Why do adults say that children's imaginations are better and more widely spread than theirs? People are the same in this respect, aren't they? Maybe not! If not maybe it's because adult's minds are older and can't think as well as children. And children's minds are just beginning. Do you think this could be the real reason?

Clarke: February 1
    It's funny how sports go along with business in a way. Business is becoming more thought than strength and baseball does the same thing. It used to be how fast a pitcher can throw the ball, now it's how good can you throw curves and sinkers and fancy things.

Oliver: February 7
    Why are some people smarter than others? Is it because of the ancestors or parents? Is it because the size of a person's brain? If yes, how can people have bigger brains than others?
    Why are some people kinder than others? Why do some people have larger emotions than others like when one person gets "D" they sort of laugh at it while another person might cry? Why do people have different personalities than others? Do kinder people usually have better personalities, do they go together or are they completely different things? This is an interesting study.

Lisa: March 6
    I wonder if a tear is real water. Couldn't it be some clear fluid secreted by the body? How can your body know when it's time to cry?

                                                                     April 11
    I wonder if some poems and songs are trying to relay a message. I know many poems that do, but I mean messages about what is wrong in the world today and yesterday. If they do relay these messages why don't people listen to them?

Doris: May 2
    I think that people who try to act more grown up than they really are are really wasting years of their life away because when they get to be the age they're trying to be it won't be any fun. And if they try to be the age

they missed when they were younger they'll look pretty silly. Why don't people just try to have fun at the age they are?

April 15

It seems like it is easier to express your love to dogs than to humans. It seems that people are always saying, "I love you" to dogs but you rarely ever hear them saying it to humans. Why?

Gwen: January 10

Today I wondered what would happen if Thomas Edison didn't invent the light bulb and no one else invented it either until 1970 after cars were invented. What would people do? Maybe they would put candles on top of their cars, two on the front and two on the back. But then I thought it couldn't be possible because if the person was driving or the wind blows hard the light on the candle would blow out. People, I know, if it was invented would use a gas lamp. In my imagination the gas lamp is invented but people won't use it. They just can't drive their cars after the sun goes down or when it is foggy out.

Sandra: February 2

I was telling Jodi a secret I had. I also told Sally, Ellen and heaven only knows who else. What it got me to thinking about is why do people always tell other people their secrets? If they want it to be a secret why do they keep on telling people? Pretty soon it will get to the person that they don't want it to get to. Boy, some people.

Keith: February 16

Why is it when you are with people all the time they start laughing over something and you don't know what they're laughing about? Why don't you know what they're laughing about? I think they have met in a place and laughed over it and then laughed over it again.

Stephen: March 15

Tuesday I was watching combat on T.V. I started thinking about how Americans on T.V. are good guys and in Germany the Germans are the good guys and the Americans are bad.

I guess all the shows on T.V. in other countries are the opposite of ours.

Susan: September 19

As I was laying in my bed thinking of what I could write next in my journal, I couldn't think of anything. So the next morning when I got up I wondered why do I do my thinking in bed. I think of it very often but not often enough to recognize that I'm thinking about it.

Gwen: February 8

Today as I was thinking of a journal entry I looked at the word "Cascade." It seemed like a funny word to me because I haven't heard it very much. I wondered how things could be invented. I tried to think of something I could invent. First I tried to invent a shape but I couldn't. Then I tried to invent something else. I couldn't do that either. I guess to invent something you have to be very intelligent.

Stephen: September 16
Today I was fixing the handle bars on my bike. Looking around, I noticed that everything was put together with nuts and bolts.

I wonder who the man was that was smart enough to think of such a simple way of putting things together?

Keith: October 7
Why do people wear white at night? Why isn't there a color that you can see better? Why can't a light blue mix together and be better to see at night than white? I think there is a lighter color than white but the people do not want to let the people have the beautiful color.

Cheryl: October 11
Did you ever look at a lady with high heels on walk? There are the types that clip clop down the stairs or that walk very dainty. Some of them stick their feet into much or stick them out like the letter "Y." I wonder how I will walk with big clumpy high heels?

Keith: October 17
Why do people that have swimming pools go to the beach? I think they go to the beach cause they want to see their friends swim. But if they went to the beach and they had a swimming pool they would be losing money.

Bonnie: October 18
When we study different bases we always establish our numerals first. That is, before we do anything else. If we were doing any base we'd always start out with zero as our first numeral. What gets me is that people call zero a numeral but they don't use it like the other numerals. So what is zero? I'd call it a symbol because it isn't like any of the other numerals. So why don't people call the whole group symbols and all except zero numerals?

Frank: October 25
Today in math I was wondering why we cannot write twelve in base twelve. In our number system we write twelve like this 12 and in base twelve it is like this   twelves|ones   so if we haven't invented 12 we can't write 2.   1 | 0

Ceceile: November 21
Today I wondered why there hasn't been a colored man to be president. Ever since George Washington has been president there hasn't been a colored man to be president. I wonder why. What's the matter with colored men?

Charles: December 7
Today when I was playing with my baby cousin I wondered why he couldn't talk. He only makes sounds that sound funny.

When I tried to make one I nearly choked trying to do it. If I sort of choked trying to make the sounds maybe he sort of chokes trying to make sounds too.

I think he choked because his throat and vocal cords aren't fully adjusted to making sounds. If it was he would be able to talk.

December 21
Today I will write some more about why I think a baby can't talk. When I sing if I go too low it makes, "another one of those funny sounds." Maybe when the baby is young its voice is pitched so low that it can't talk. As the child grows its pitch grows and it can talk. Or at least that's what I think.

Lorraine: January 11
Today in math Mr. Jacobs was doing several division problems when the class was disturbed by his mistakes. When he found them he said to the class that today wasn't his day. I believed him. But today was a pretty good day for me. Why are some days good for some people and not good for others? I really don't know do you?

Gwen: January 17
Why do countries write treaties if nothing happens when you do something against it? It really doesn't mean anything. It's just like making a promise and if you want you can break it. The reason countries might sign this is because they think the other country won't break it.

Gretchen: January 27
How come white people think Negroes are crazy for doing what they do when white people do just as much stuff? Or is it that white people don't like Negroes and Negroes don't like us?

January 25
When scientists find a germ why don't they find something about the germ before naming it some fancy hard and long word? And when they tell somebody they will use words that they don't clearly understand and expect other people to.

Susan: October 20
How come when you lean next to some bricks your hair catches on? I know they have little holes in them. But how can your hair stick in? Also it could be by friction because when you get your hair off it's all fuzzy.

Gwen: April 3
Over the Easter vacation I got a kite. When I was through putting it together I flew it. It got torn in a few places so I taped it up. When I went to fly it again it didn't fly high at all. My brother said the tape made it too heavy. I wondered how tape could hold a kite down. When I hold tape it doesn't weigh a thing. Maybe weight is different up in the air.

Theresa: March 15
Today I was wondering why sometimes when you go someplace and you don't get home till real later, you get all tired and by the time you're in bed you're not tired any more. This happens every time I stay up real late or whenever I'm just plain real tired. Is it because by the time you're ready for bed you've wakened yourself up? If this is so why can't you get tired the same way you get wakened?

Craig: March 8
When I was pouring water over the faucet I noticed that the water went in a straight line (followed in a line). Why? Well I think on the faucet there are particles of dust and other stuff. When a drop of water goes down the faucet it makes a path for the other water. I mean the drop of water pushes the dust away and makes a water way for the other water.

Theresa: January 9
Today I was wondering how lightning has electricity in it. Lightning comes from the sky and it seems odd to have electricity coming from the sky even though you get used to it. When it rains the water might help the electricity in the lightning but I don't understand how we get lightning in the summer without any water if the water does help.

Bill: November 15
Today while we were riding in the car it dawned on me that there was simply no reason that round things roll and square things don't. I tried to come to a conclusion and got this one: Flat things don't roll because one-fourth of the object is on the ground but only a small fraction of a round thing is on the ground at once.

Susan: February 15
One of the hardest things to do on the patrols that I have found is . . . . When there is no talking on the bus and you find one of your real close friends are in the middle of the bus and they are talking to their friends I find it hard to scream and say, "Judy stop talking." I mean, "quiet down." Something happens so that you can hardly say anything.

Keith: June 12
Why is it when you run up for a fly ball it seems to jump up and down? Why? Why does this happen? I think when you run up you go up and then you come down and as you do this you think the ball is jumping.

Gwen: May 1
Today I wondered why it is that when you do the work you like you're not tired until you stop working. I wondered why.
I thought maybe this was because you're doing the work you like but don't realize you're doing too much. When you stop working it's a quick change from working too much and resting.

Ceceile: January 26
Today when I was on the bus taking patrol, Tony dropped his lunch and I picked it up. Then he said, "Thank you" and I said, "You're welcome."
I used to think that "welcome" means to come in when you're invited or something. Then I said you're welcome and it seems to me that I said that you're welcome to come to my house. That's what I used to think and I still do.
Maybe they have two different meanings. They just can't because they are spelled alike.

Gretchen: April 4
When girl meets boy and boy kisses girl does that mean they love or are
they going to get married or what?
Why do movie stars only marry rich and famous people? The way
everybody's getting rich who is going to marry the ugly and poor people?

Alan: June 1
Today I heard a boy tell another boy that on Friday in your lunch you
would get a free ice cream. I heard Mr. Jacobs say it too. I thought about
it and thought that the ice cream is part of the lunch and you pay for it
when you pay for your lunch. Most everybody says it is free but it is not
free.

Olga: March 17
I have noticed that when you come across an older group of kids they
usually seem to put on a show when they notice you. Sometimes they just
want to attract attention from other people that come near. Or they just
like to kid or fool around. But sometimes when they do this they like to
show off in front of people and think that they are great. But when the
younger kids see them they usually stop and watch them. But when they
stop and watch the older ones seem to fool around longer. Probably they
want to give the other kids more entertainment.

Susan: January 17
It seems like time is always going different three different ways. One
way is it will be 5:00 and you iron your dress and it will be 8:30. Another
way is the older you get the faster time goes. Still another way is when
you want to go some place and you're all ready and you have an hour to
go but when you're in a hurry time goes so quickly. This journal is not a
question and time won't ever change but it seems that way!

Betsy: October 10
When you look at an object for a good while and then close your eyes
you can still see it (except blurry). Maybe this is because when you see and
when you close your eyes you still see it because you're thinking about
seeing it. I don't really know why this happens but try it and see if it
works.

Gladys: November 28
Last night while I was lying in bed I rubbed my eyes. I stopped rubbing
them and they were still closed. I saw little funny designs. I wondered how
I could see this with my eyes closed. Is it that all your thoughts gather in
your mind and it's like a tape recorder on your eye lids and you see it
instead of hearing it? Or are you just looking into your mind?

Gwen: November 4
Today I wondered how it is when you look at something bright and
then you close your eyes you still see the same thing but it is a different
color. This happened to me before I looked at my window and then closed
my eyes and I saw it but it was purple.

Betsy: November 16

When you look at things how can you be so sure its a color? Maybe our eyes are just seeing colors that aren't there. Maybe everything is black or brown.

Yolanda: April 21

Today I started wondering if what I see as red is really the same color you see? My brother and I talked about this before and I really don't believe it, but it could be possible. Even if people all see a different color for red, they have learned that it is called r-e-d. My brother and I tried to describe colors to each other, but without much luck. But he must see differently than I do because he said black is a bright color and that white looks like a real light gray.

Nancy: October 10

Some times I wonder when you close your eyes real tight you see colors. Why do you see them when your eyes are closed?

Quentin: November 3

It's my father's birthday today and I'm thinking why people celebrate birthdays. So you're a year older. Big deal. A year of your life is gone. I don't think that you should celebrate birthdays.

Margaret:

I am thinking back to my birthday. I was 11. I don't feel any older or look any older. I think that if I had my way I think every person would change in at least one way on their birthday. It would make me feel a lot better.

Clarke: February 6

When you do something good and you get compliments it's hard to stay modest. You try but inside you want to say I know it was good or something like that.

Lisa: March 8

I wonder why people when they are given praise always say what they've done is icky or horrible. Deep down inside they know what they've done is good but why are they ashamed to say so?

Sandra: March 1

Today when we were doing buttermilk art some people told me that my picture was good. I said I don't think so and I meant it. Some people say it to make people say it again but I didn't. I heard somebody (I won't mention the name) say, "She's just conceited. All she wants is attention." People always think just the opposite of what is the truth.

May 3

When Mr. Jacobs finished reading my journal I commented on it and said it was nutty. How can I say my own journal is nutty? If I wrote it I can't say it's stupid. But the more I think about it the more I'm against it. Not many people wake up at 2:00 AM. That's why I think it's so stupid.

Cheryl: October 24
Do you ever notice that when you are mad at someone you blame it on
someone else? Today I was cross with my mother so I blamed it on a
friend. I seemed to holler at her for no reason at all. I then wondered why
I got cross with her. She had not done anything to me. I thought maybe I
did not want to blame myself so instead I got angry with her.

Gwen: March 22
Today I wondered when you get mad at a friend you stay mad for a
pretty long time but when you get mad at a brother or sister you don't
stay mad long at all. I thought maybe this was because you live with your
brother or sister and you just can't stay mad for long because you're
always with them.

Olga: March 8
Some times I have wondered why my sister gets me all excited about
something. Things like when she has candy or cookies. But when she does
this to me she really doesn't have these things. But when she says this it
sounds like she really has these things. I have wondered why she does this
to me? She said the reason why she does this is she likes to kid me. But the
real reason is because when she tells me these things I always fall for it. I
really go along with thinking that she really had these goodies. Also she
said that it is so easy to get me excited.

Cheryl: January 26
When I go away to camp it seems that I never have time to miss my
parents. I think my parents think more about me than I do of them. I am
either horseback riding, swimming, fishing, hiking, shooting bows and ar-
rows or rifles, or playing games. I really don't have time to miss my
parents. Don't you agree?
I thought and wondered why I don't miss them and they miss me. That
seemed very easy to answer since when my parents go away I miss them
because they aren't at the dinner table and they don't kiss me good night.
The answer to my thought must be because I am playing and having a
good time but my parents have time to miss me because I am not at the
dinner table and they don't have a chance to holler.

Sandra: October 10
When we went on our forestry hike today Mr. Dengler told us that once
a tree has grown a certain height it won't grow anymore from that place.
(Below will be a picture.) I don't see how this can be. Why does just one
part of a tree grow up and out when the other part just grows out? I don't
see how this can happen.

Charles: October 6
Today in forestry I wondered why one given spot on a tree never
moves. I think that if a given spot was on the top of the tree and was still
growing, I think that the spot would keep being pushed up and up by the
tree.
On the C & O hike I wondered about the trees with the
funny branches. I think that the trunk was pushed to one side
somehow. But the branches still wanted to grow straight like
this:

Mona: December 14
In the daytime if you look far away into the sky it is light blue and if you look straight up you see a darker blue. The sky isn't deeper in some places than in others is it? Also when you're outside you're really in the sky but it isn't blue. Why? Why is the sky darker in outer space?

Jennifer: March 1
I know that all people are different but do they all have feelings? I thought they did but maybe some people are born without feelings. The most horrible loss to suffer, I would think, would be a loss of feelings.

Suzanne: May 18
Today I realized that kids don't know the good things in life. They don't think something is very much fun but after they do it for awhile they begin to like it. Take square dancing at Mar-Lu-Ridge for instance. Only a few of us wanted to square dance at the beginning, but at the end everyone wanted to keep dancing.
I wonder if grownups do any stupid things like that?

Bonnie: March 22
I got another idea about people seeing different colors and how this might effect someone's career. Suppose you have someone who attempted to be a painter but failed. This person can paint terrific as far as balance, the way something looks realistic, and things like that are concerned. The reason this person was rejected was because of how he painted in colors. Thousands of people might see colors the same but he could be an exception. Suppose he saw all the colors that the other people saw as dark and dull colors as bright and cheery colors. If this was so he might paint a picture using colors he thought bright but colors the critics thought outlandish. This might explain a painter not succeeding in his chosen career.

Doris: April 5
Why do people try to be "in"? Why don't they just try to be kinder?

                                                        April 8
I think that people who are "in" are soon going to be "out" because nobody else will like them when their "in" group breaks up.

Bonnie: November 8
What makes the mind work? How does it happen? One thing that really gets me is how it stores its information. That is, I know it stores it in its cells. But how? I mean, how is the information recorded in the cells? It's probably hard to understand what I'm saying. You could say I'm asking if the information is recorded in something like writing form.